VIA FOLIOS 111

The Story of My People

The Story of My People

From Rural Southern Italy to Mainstream America

Mario B. Mignone

BORDIGHERA PRESS

Library of Congress Control Number: 2015937924

Printed in the United States.

Published by
BORDIGHERA PRESS
John D. Calandra Italian American Institute
25 West 43rd Street, 17th Floor
New York, NY 10036

VIA FOLIOS 111
ISBN 978-1-59954-089-4

TABLE OF CONTENTS

ACKNOWLEDGEMENTS

Where do I start to make acknowledgments in a book like this, built on a myriad of experiences, observations, impressions, and reflections? My first and most important thanks go to my parents and siblings who shared, for the most part, my immigrant experience and shaped in great measure the first stage of my life. My huge extended family played an almost equally important role in molding our early American experience and helped in pouring the foundation for the realization of the American dream; to all of them I feel a sense of gratitude. And to Lois, my extraordinary wife of forty-seven years, and to my exceptional daughters, Pamela Saltzman, Cristina Armato, and Elizabeth Jakic, my deep love and affection for having tolerated my character shaped by growing up through the hardships of a very destructive war, of living in a family of eight siblings, and living the immigrant experience.

I also would like to take the opportunity to thank my City College friends of the Italian Club, immigrants like me who, while working full-time at jobs, sought the promises and opportunities of the American Dream. My dream and their dreams have been followed by the dreams of the new immigrants from India, China, Korea, Philippines, Africa who have the same desires and aspirations supported by the same strong work ethic — to them too my gratitude for having inspired me to tell this story of immigration.

I must not forget to mention that the idea of this book first originated from the strong desire of two nephews of mine, John Mignone and Michael Amato, to know the immigrant story of their family and pushed me write about "our" experience. The idea was also nourished by a dear friend of the family, the Honorable Senator Kenneth LaValle, who showed a great interest in learning more about our process to mainstream America.

In bringing this work to conclusion, I had the immense good fortune to have the attention of Stan Pugliese, Bill Boelhower, and Fred Gardaphé, extraordinary scholars and creative writers, who read the text carefully and made substantial suggestions. I cannot forget the moral voice of my friend, the Reverend Doctor Calvin Butts, an extraordinary university administrator and exceptional civic leader.

My wife Lois and my sister–in-law Sheila Mignone read the entire manuscript with the keen eyes of language teachers who have exceptional feeling for words; the book benefited from their readings.

My gratitude goes to Sian Gibby, Communications Publications Writer of the John D. Calandra Italian American Institute, who invested energy and passion in the production of this work. Her skills and creativity are evident in the shape and content of the final product. But this book would not have been possible without the strong interest and the enthusiastic support of the Editor, Anthony Julian Tamburri, who embraced and promoted the idea from beginning to end. Hearty thanks to you, Anthony.

THE STORY OF MY PEOPLE

From Rural Southern Italy to Mainstream America

ONE

We all feel inspired to display our favorite photographs about the house or collect them in an album in an attempt to capture what we consider the most important moments of our lives and give them some sense of order and narrative coherence. They remind us of who we are, where we come from, and what is dear to us. They usually do. And so we keep them in the most prominent places of our living room and where we work. We even carry them with us wherever we go—for example, in our wallet with our money! I remember, when I was a child, my paternal grandmother carried close to her heart the picture of her son who had emigrated to America many years before and had never come back.

In my study I have a picture that represents a defining moment in my family's life. There are many moments that could be considered thresholds in our lives, and some are traumatic and others joyful. The picture I am now looking at on my desk was taken in front of St. Peter's in Rome the day we emigrated to the United States. It's a picture that says so much about that day, the history of our family up to that point, and our Southern Italian culture.

There we stood, posing as a group, all of us part of the same sweeping drama, each seemingly locked in one's own sad thoughts. It was a large group of twenty-five, mostly family members and some very close friends. My father had rented a small bus to take the eight of us to the airport and had decided to invite some relatives and close friends along to see us off. Some of those people are now gone, and with them part of our history. The picture was taken to capture a spot in time: family and friends in front of St. Peter's before separating forever. Yes, forever, for those in the group never got together again, and some of them we would never see again, after that last moment in Rome. Looking at the picture, I can still feel the mood of that day: nobody smiling, nobody laughing, no one with a light heart. We were all conscious that it was not a simple goodbye. When one emigrates and crosses the ocean, there is an overwhelming sense that nothing will ever be the same again. If anything, emigration means being uprooted at every level imaginable—psychological, cultural, and, hopefully, economic.

There she is, *Nonna* Maria, my paternal grandmother. She is standing and is dressed in her usual black, with a shawl on her head and arms crossed over her stomach. Since the loss of her husband, *Nonno* Enrico, about thirty years before, she started to dress in black in sign of mourning and never dared wear any other color again. This was last time I saw her.

My father's oldest brother, *Zio* Agostino, is there and his eyes seem to be fixed on me with a sense of disappointment at our leaving—perhaps because he did not have children of his own. He was very attached to us and we to him. I also think, however, that he was hoping in his heart that we would be successful over there, in the new world. We remained very attached to *Zio* Agostino, and that bond of affection was never broken. Years later, in his will he expressed his love and pride for us by leaving everything he owned to us "Americans" and in a language that was deeply moving.

In the same photograph my brother Enrico, twenty-two years old, the oldest of the siblings and bearing my paternal grandfather's name, seems perplexed. He was not leaving with us because he was enrolled in medical school in Genoa and he had no idea what he was going to do when he graduated: join the family in America or stay home and practice medicine in Italy, enjoying the prestige that no one in my family had achieved before?

My father in the back row is apparently even more perplexed, for he was sending his wife and seven children—from the ages of four to twenty—to America while he remained in Italy. And nobody, including him, knew when he would be able to join us. The separation and the overwhelming sense of uncertainty it caused were making the departure even more painful and tense.

My siblings were lined up in front of my father according to height. In the front is Agnese, four years old and bearing my maternal grandmother's name; Domenico, eight years old and named after my father's brother, who had passed away the year before my brother was born; next to him is Biagio, almost ten, and named after my maternal grandfather who was waiting for us in America. Then there is Nino, almost thirteen, who was given the name of my mother's brother, Gioacchino, who was called Nino for short and had passed away many years before at a young age; and then Maria, fifteen, named after my paternal grandmother; and finally, Matilde, the oldest after me, who was almost eighteen and was named after my maternal great-grandmother.

True, by emigrating we were abandoning so much that was intimately part of our lives, but we were also carrying off a part of the family history, along with memories steeped in the values of our Southern Italian culture. The names we were carrying across the ocean were deeply rooted in our family history and reflected centuries-old traditions. A name bestowed upon a child is probably the first gift that parents give to their children, but in our Southern Italian culture, until the 1970s, it was a choice that followed well-established practices. My parents closely followed those practices. No name of my siblings was chosen because it sounded melodious, or connected with an historic or mythological figure, or reflected the love for a movie or sports star. Nothing like that. Names had to connect with our past and bring the past into the future. Names are like property (in fact, "*Proprietà Mignone*" is chiseled in stone in our ancestral house). Going to America, with our names we were bringing some of our history with us and some important traditions.

But back to that picture, which has the air of a funeral. In those years, the drama of emigration, with its final goodbyes, was often seen as equivalent to death. When I look at the picture in front of St. Peter's, inevitably I remember the trip from Benevento to Rome, the flight over the ocean, and our arrival in New York. But I am not nostalgic about it. Although we had all been waiting many years for that day, none of us enjoyed the frustration and the burden of that dream.

That trip into the unknown scared all of us, and for different reasons we were also sad that my father and my oldest brother were not traveling with us. Having already completed his first year of medical school at the University of Genoa, my brother Enrico, with the blessing of my parents, had wisely decided to remain in Italy to continue his studies. My father instead was staying back because he had no other choice. He was a victim of the Cold War syndrome. The American Consulate had received compromising political information gathered from the background check to which he as a potential emigrant was subjected. My father had been labeled a Socialist!

Because of this political stigma our departure was delayed for about six years. During those years we had been kept in the dark, waiting in a sort of limbo. It seems that the local *carabinieri*, in response to the American Consulate's questionnaire, had stated that my father belonged to a family of Socialists, a dangerous species in those years of the Cold War. For six years, with passports ready, we were denied departure visas for political reasons — without our knowing anything about it! The knot was untied in the summer of 1960, the summer of the Rome Olympics, when my grandmother, *Zio* Vincenzo, and *Zia* Flora came to Italy from America. *Zia* Flora, a strong-willed woman, had the courage to go to the American Consulate and ask why we were not given our visas. The forthcoming revelation was a mixture of shock, surprise, and consternation. "Did you ever meet my brother-in-law?" she asked. "Do you really believe that he is able to bring the Socialist revolution to the U.S.? His only desire is to provide a better future for his family. Believe me. The only thing that my brother-in-law can do is manual labor. He doesn't have an ideology; he doesn't know what Socialism is." And in fact my father was not an ideologue; he was a simple, hard-working farmer. As a farmer and with a fifth-grade education he had only a vague idea of what political parties stood for. For a while he was a member of the Liberal Party, and then, when he started to suspect that we were not getting our visas for political reasons, he became a member of the Christian Democratic Party. He had sensed that his brother Egidio's militancy in the Socialist Party was compromising his own reputation in the village and clearly wanted to clarify his political affiliation. But apparently to no avail.

The authorities at the American Consulate did not give in to my aunt's insistence, but they became more malleable when my aunt said that the misrepresentation of my father's political representation should not unfairly punish the rest of the family. "If you are truly afraid that my brother-in-law will bring a revolution to America, keep him here and allow my sister and her children to come to America." The proposal was perceived as a fair request, but splitting up the family in this way would create another problem: "Who is going to support a family of seven children, the oldest age twenty and the youngest four years old?" It was a legitimate question. "America cannot open the doors to immigrants who are going on welfare as soon they arrive," an authoritative voice scolded my aunt. "No one of us is on welfare," she answered back, "we don't even know what welfare is. We work very hard and are willing and able to support them." — "OK, if you are able and willing to support them, show us that you are financially fit and your sister and children will get the visa." In two weeks' time we went through the health and physical tests, were given visas, and were ready to leave.

My father quickly got busy preparing our departure. He was proud that he did not have to sell any property to buy the eight air tickets and to purchase the needed clothing for going to America. On September 8, early in the morning, we left for Rome. Because a car was not large enough for all of us and our luggage, my father rented a bus. It was an incredible decision. He knew very well that the departure was not going to be easy for us, so he had the bright idea to ask some of our relatives and close friends to come with us to the airport. My grandmother, Uncle Agostino, my aunt Italia and two of her children, and a few more relatives joined us. I had also invited a couple of my closest friends from high school.

The trip to Rome was somber. We chatted about generalities and a lot of the time we just stared outside to find refuge in the landscape. I was looking at those hills and mountains with mixed feelings. I had read the beautiful pages of "*Addio ai monti*" of Lucia in *I promessi sposi/The Betrothed*, by Alessandro Manzoni. The pathos and sadness of that departure compared to the sadness of departing emigrants was not matching my feelings. Riding in the bus, I too cast a melancholy look behind at the mountains, hills, and the rest of the landscape, illumined by the early rays of the sun, and varied by multitudes of shadows. There they were, small villages, houses, cottages so familiar to my eyes. There it was, our house, on top of the hill with the huge birch tree in front. It was unquestionably a melancholy sight. They were all places as known to me as the faces of friends! Every site, every sound was as familiar as the faces and voices of my family. I had seen and heard them since my infancy! I was saying my farewell to them without crying or a sigh. It was a departure without remorse. And now I was driven from them by an adverse fate with scarce hope of return!

That land had not been generous, and a great number of people had to leave in search of better living opportunities. Yes, the landscape was beautiful; in fact, it was amazing; so picturesque. But people could barely survive on it. If I did not leave for America, I would have left for sure for other destinations. My brother Enrico and I had already made an attempt at leaving. When I was sixteen, I had applied for the Italian Air Force Academy and had been "rejected" at the physical test, like so many other thousands of kids. Enrico had applied at age 18 for the school of Officers of Carabinieri; and he suffered the same fate. In those years no door would open without the right push. But now, we were leaving for real. We were pushed by a natural yearning to be better off. Like a great tide, as it had done for millions of people in our region, the current of progress swept us away. We were hoping to say good-bye to the unglamorous years of trials and tribulations endured by my family.

Our departure was part of a century-old human flow. I had heard stories of emigrants, I had seen friends and neighbors leaving. Emigration had been part of our daily experience; I must say, of a painful experience even by the way emigration and emigrants had been regarded or, even worse, disregarded. As a student, I had never read a page in our textbooks that recalled the sacrifice of emigrants. Not a page, not a chapter, not a lesson had ever been devoted to emigration, as if it did not exist, as if Italy were ashamed of those Italians who had left the *patria* in search of *benessere* elsewhere. Yet I and many of my classmates had been touched profoundly by emigration; we had relatives in numerous parts of the world and were eager to learn about their destiny. I had my maternal grandparents, uncles, aunts, and cousins in America but their sacrifices were not recorded in any of our textbooks. As a child I remember getting up very early in the morning to say the last goodbyes to the *paesani* and friends leaving for distant lands, many of them for Australia in those years. I remember the cries and the painful embraces of separation that we carried silently within us, entombed in our hearts for many years. I still remember how we, as children, would talk about the departure of our friends and wonder whether we were ever going to see them; again, however, in the classroom there was never a composition to express our pain or to comment on our losses.

Now it was our turn. I knew why I was leaving but I didn't know what I was going to do, and when and if I would come back. I was feeling the pain of the rupture, but I was not feeling that anything was pulling me back. I was moving more because of the force of expulsion than by the force of attraction. America's mythology was not beaming and luring me with joy. It was more the conviction that to free ourselves from the oppressive living conditions on a desolated farm we had to move. If we did not get the visa, I had already planned to leave for Northern Italy and become part of the Southern human flow to the North. I could feel the fire in my belly to start my adult life away from home in an urban setting.

I had a sense that the uprooting was for good. I was not driven by a desire to go away to make money and come back and go to live on those hills again hopefully as a rich American. That was not part of my dream. And now that I was leaving, I was looking at those hills and mountains with intense conviction that a part of my life was being left back without the hope or desire to reconnect with it again sometime in the future. The sunrises and sunsets on those hills, although beautiful, were only going to be alive and relived in my memory.

Because all of us, including our friends, had never been outside of Benevento, my father had planned a stop in Rome before proceeding for the airport. We had a sightseeing tour: the Coliseum, the Roman Forum, Piazza Venezia, and St. Peter's. At St. Peter's we got off the bus and visited the basilica. It was an amazing sight. Everything was interesting but we lacked excitement to appreciate it: no expressions of wonder, surprise, exhilaration. We took some pictures; but they were not taken to record the momentous visit of a bunch of tourists in front of a building that represented the essence of our faith. All my brothers and sisters still display prominently in some place of their homes a copy of that group picture in front of St. Peter's. It's a photo that presents a frozen moment, an impression in time. Today, from those impressions arise a myriad of thoughts. After so many years I can still read in the expression of those faces the feelings in each of us.

We all have in our homes pictures that have recorded special moments in our lives, happy or sad moments, and occasionally we look at them and our memory brings up some reflections. For me there is no other picture that elicits more reflection: It gives a reading of the hearts and minds of us emigrants at the moment of separation—the traumatic cutting of the umbilical cord. The feelings in that image stay with us; are carried on into the ethers of space and time.

That picture says so much about my state of mind. I was wondering when I was going to see my friends again and, even more troubling, if I ever was going to see my grandmother again. She was there with us, silent, as if part of a funeral procession. She and we were conscious of her age and the distance that was going to separate us. At a certain point, she gained courage and uttered a few words: "You are a big boy now and are strong enough to work, but be careful and keep an eye on your brothers and sisters. America is so big and these children are still so small." It wasn't just the words that pinched my stomach, but the grave tone of those words that stirred my mind. I knew that I was the oldest of the seven and that I had to assume some responsibilities, but I had not given any thoughts to what degree I was expected to be the big brother. Those words were like a testament: I never saw my *nonna* again, but the echo of those words resounded in my mind for many years. When we arrived at the airport we embraced each other and said goodbye with few tears. My mother was crying openly and so was little sister Agnese. I wanted to give the impression of being already strong; I took two suitcases, said to my brothers and sister *"Andiamo"* and led the way inside the airport.

The flight to New York on a DC8, a propeller, was very long. We had left Rome in the evening, and had stopped in the middle of the night in Shannon, to refuel. In the six-hour flight, we had not been able to close our eyes. The propeller flying in the clouds had not offered a smooth ride; many people had to use the bags available in the pockets in front of our seats. Agnese had cried for most of the time partially because she was scared to be on the plane, and partially because she was missing my father. She was only four years old and, understandably, could not figure out why we had left for so far without my father. The mood of the rest of the family, of my mother and of my other five siblings, was certainly not reassuring to her. My mother had tried her best to distract her by telling stories, but the faces of her brothers and sisters were not conveying any sense of joy or cheerful expectations.

After a short stop in Shannon in the middle of the night, and after having wandered like lost birds in the ghostly airport, we were again on the Alitalia DC8 for New York. The twelve-hour flight to cross the Atlantic was as bumpy and full of anxiety as the six hours from Rome. That was the first time we were on a plane; for that matter my brothers and sisters had never even been on a train. Traveling had not been part of our culture, and now on a plane, closed in like chickens in a coop, the trip was very distressing. We had nothing to do and nothing to say to each other. Boredom only exacerbated the anxiety of flying. No one had given us advice on how to prepare for the flight; but who could have done it? Our farmer friends, our sheep and goats? Some reading material, a book or a magazine, probably would have helped. On the other hand, reading wasn't our thing, nor were crossword puzzles.

My mother again tried to entertain Agnese by telling fables and short stories. Mamma was an extraordinary storyteller and succeeded to distract her to the point that she relaxed and fell asleep. The rest of the siblings spent the time trying to rest by staring through the windows of the plane or daydreaming. The boys, Nino, Biagio, and Domenico, were seated in the same row and, because of boredom, were constantly bickering. At one point, tired of their nuisance and complaints to my mother about the pinching and elbowing of one to the other, I intervened. "I will break your heads if you don't stop." To put annoyance to an end, I asked Nino to move to my seat and I moved between the other two. It never came to my mind that for three boys, age thirteen, ten, and eight, a flight of eighteen hours was too much to bear. These were boys that had grown up on top of a hill where they could move like birds: climb trees, run through open fields. Here they were now, as in a pigeon coop. Finally, once they had been separated in their seats, overcome by dullness, they fell asleep.

I, instead, was fully alert and thinking about what was really happening. My grandmother's words were bouncing in my head. I was going to America as an emigrant: to join some family members — maternal grandparents, some cousins, and my mother's two brothers and a sister — but mainly I was going to work, just the way my grandfather had done fifty-three years before and many millions of other emigrants had done for generations. However, I was trying to convince myself that I was emigrating to a very different America, and, in many respects, our voyage to America *was* different. I was trying to find comfort in the fact that our trip in a plane was a picnic compared to the trips by ship taken by my grandfather many times. I knew very well the story of those crossings and those of many emigrants who had crossed the Atlantic by ship in the lowest-class passage available, the steerage, a trip that took about two weeks, with hundreds of people of different nationalities sharing quarters under conditions not much better than those that they had left behind. On the plane I was trying to find consolation in the fact that we did not have to deal with unhealthy conditions and endless seasickness experienced on ships by previous generations of emigrants. So many were weakened to the point of death. We were going to America in a DC8 and we were dressed decorously. My parents had bought for each of us a new outfit; we had never been dressed in such a generous way. We were emigrants, no doubt; we were still taking the voyage for economic reasons like the relatives who had preceded us, but we had achieved some respectable level of education and probably were better prepared to face the challenges of the uprooting than my relatives who had emigrated before us.

Notwithstanding this awareness, which should have put me in a zone of comfort, I was scared. During the flight I did not close my eyes. The fear of the unknown was too big. I was twenty and the oldest of my siblings. My sister Matilde, next in line, was almost eighteen, and Maria was fifteen. I was aware that it was impossible for my mother to go to work: She had a full-time job at home taking care of the needs of the *new* family of eight. I knew that I had to go to work immediately and I didn't have a problem with that, but I did not know how I was going to realize the American dream. If Matilde could find work and Maria chipped in with a part-time job, we were going to make it.

Suddenly I was the head of this family without having sought it and without any preparation. The American Consulate, by not allowing my father to emigrate, was enforcing a policy aimed at protecting America from the infiltration of the Reds, but it was throwing my family into uncharted seas, and no one was a seasoned seaman. It was not the flight that was bothering me; it was the anxiety of the arrival that was distressing.

We had been told that *Zio* Gaetano, my mother's brother, was going to meet us at the airport. *Zio* Vincenzo had given me twenty dollars for an emergency. In case *Zio* Gaetano did not show up, I had the money and the phone number to call him up. While landing, I checked in my pocket to make sure that I still had the twenty dollar bill and the phone number. I felt distinctively the two different papers and felt reassured. I had never dialed a phone number in my life and was hoping that I did not have to do it as my first test of my encounter with America. On top of that anxiety, I was worried how Uncle Gaetano was going to pick us up at the airport; how he was going to handle eight people plus their luggage? My father had rented a bus to take us to the airport! I had seen in the movies that in America everything was big, some of the cars huge compared to Italian standards, but not even a truck could have handled all of us and our belongings.

When we landed we were all in a daze. The lack of sleep, the stress of the long flight, the anxiety of the arrival, the cultural shock of a new reality, all were taking a toll on us. I cannot remember how we carried out all our luggage. I am certain however, that we did not ask the help of a porter. After our encounter with the custom agents, much more inquisitive then than now, we moved outside. In the sea of people waiting for relatives and friends it was not easy to connect with a face we knew. "Guys, look well," I said to Nino and Biagio, "he is very tall and has red hair." There we were, looking intensely, analyzing every face. After a while they all looked the same! "There he is," said Domenico, pointing to a tall man with olive skin. "Where," I asked. "There," he said. "Stupid, didn't I say that he has red hair." And we continued to look in that sea of people where people's faces had increasingly lost their uniqueness. The fear that my uncle was not there was blurring my vision even more, and the concern about the twenty dollars Uncle Vincent had given me in case we had to take a taxi was even stronger. Suddenly, I heard my mother scream: "Gaetano." I imagine that the scream was not just to get the attention of my uncle but probably more to reassure my brothers and sisters that we had anchored properly, that we had connected with America. I could feel a sigh of relief from all of us.

My uncle embraced each one of us and then introduced us to his second cousin, Uncle Gelsomino, who had come to help the pickup with his station wagon. After the customary ceremony of greetings and questions on our flight, they went to the parking lot to get the cars while we waited for them at the curb. We were breathing the American air with a sense of relief. The sight was so different from what we were accustomed to. The America that we had seen on the screens, the America of the cowboys that had fascinated me for so many years, was still part of a dream. What I was seeing was not connecting with my image of America.

TWO

We loaded half of the luggage into Uncle Guy's huge Buick. The car was so big that there was room even for a sheep or a goat, if we had brought one. The other half of the suitcases were loaded in Uncle Gelsomino's station wagon; that, too, was a huge car. It was the beginning of what constantly became an adjustment of view of normality: As the big cars became part of our normality, we quickly learned that everything else was big, the hamburgers the Americans ate, the Coke they drank, the clothes they wore. It did not take too long to realize that many things were defined by jumbo sizes.

My mother and the three girls settled in with Uncle Guy; the three boys and I joined Uncle Gelsomino in the station wagon. I sat in front, the boys in the back: We were five and yet were floating in the huge car. The boys could have lain across the back seat if they wanted, and they tried to get a sense of what to do with such a huge space in a car. They were very excited and were jumping up and down on the back seat; it seemed that they had already forgotten the ordeal of breaking the knot. It was clear that for them the uprooting was not going to be as traumatic as for the older siblings.

The trip from the airport to the Bronx was uneventful. Uncle Gelsomino and I tried to chat. He asked about the flight, my father, and his father who came on the bus with us to Rome. I answered his inquiries casually because I was looking out the window and trying to absorb what my eyes were able to catch from the speeding station wagon. I was still overwhelmed by the size of the cars; riding in the station wagon felt like being in a boat. Uncle Gelsomino realized my amazement and suddenly said, "This is America, big highways, big cars, skyscrapers, and big bridges." In fact, we had reached the Whitestone Bridge—there it was, unbelievably big in front of us; the aerial appearance caught my eyes. It was the most beautiful monumental steel creation I had ever seen. Crossing it, I had the impression of flying again; it gave a vivid impression of airiness and of being afloat on the Long Island Sound. Between its low railings and threadlike, widely spaced trusses, the main span suddenly opened out on a panoramic sweep of marine landscape over which the motorist has an illusion of flying. In the distance, we could see a close-knit, private community, which resembled a fishing village with its picturesque wooden bungalows along narrow lanes. Out on the point of the peninsula, beneath the towering section, there were small houses on the beach. "Turn to the left," said Uncle Gelsomino, "do you see Manhattan?"

Manhattan, whose skyscrapers seemed to be cut at their crowns by the smog, appeared disconcertingly unidentifiable. But there it was, Manhattan, the America we had seen so many times in books, on postcards, on TV screens, and movies. The America that we had dreamed of for so long was before us. There it was, standing in the distance. I kept looking as if I could penetrate it with my sight. The boys in the back were still looking with amazement at the huge bridge, the long span, and the water. "Guys, look the skyscrapers…. there, far in the distance" I said. They moved to the left side of the car and stared in the distance squashing their noses on the glass of the window. After a short while Domenico remarked with disappointment "I thought skyscrapers were so big." "They are big, stupid," Nino quickly intervened, "They are very far from here, that's why they appear small." "If we get closer I don't think they will be as big as they showed them on television," answered Domenico. And they continued bickering about how big the American skyscrapers really were.

"This is the Bronx, the borough where you will be living," said Uncle Gelsomino, "We will be home in about fifteen minutes. We must go to the very end of the Bronx. It is a nice residential area…. But there are no jobs there. You must seek work elsewhere…. Did your Uncle find a job for you?" "No, I don't think so," I answered softly. "Well, in America, you will make it only if you work hard," he said with an assertive tone; "Here, there are no secrets for success... work, work, work; that's why they want people that are physically fit." Even though I knew that and I had come mentally prepared to work, those words were very intimidating. Yes, I must admit it: I was frightened. I could not speak English, except for a few words and some formal expressions and, even worse, I did not have a skill. "I don't think you would like to work in construction where many Italians work; you are not physically strong enough, anyhow, for that job," Uncle Gelsomino said in a lower tone. "Don't worry; it will not be difficult to find a job in a factory."

The American Dream had just been reduced to work, work, work: Those words were bouncing in my mind. Work in construction or a factory. It could have also been in a pizza place or in a restaurant; after all, that's what many Italians were doing when they arrived here. Suddenly I realized, in my first encounter with America, that the views I had on the ideals of the American Dream were perceived differently by our relative. Was Uncle Gelsomino re-defining them? The American Dream used to be a shared set of ideals: the opportunity to make something of yourself; freedom to think, worship, and speak your mind; and the elevation of the common man through hard work. This country, as far as I knew, had not fallen into the dividing trap of an aristocracy and a peasant class. In America, people freely elected their leaders. They had input into how they were governed, and they would be responsible for themselves rather than depending on the shifting and wavering benevolence of a king or politicians. I had learned in high school that Americans cherished four basic principles: freedom of speech and expression, the freedom of every person to worship God in his own way, freedom from want, freedom from fear. I was probably thinking Uncle Gelsomino was right, work had to be in the forefront: It was through work that I was going to put food on the table for my family not through the idealistic principles of freedom. The image of a factory was bouncing in my mind.

We arrived at 242nd Street and White Plains Road. The buildings in the area were mostly dwellings of five apartments. We stopped in front of one, and Uncle Gelsomino said, "Here we are;

these are your grandfather's buildings." He pointed to two five-story apartment buildings. Uncle Gaetano had just arrived, and my mother and sisters were already on the sidewalk in front of a single-family house next to the two buildings. My grandfather, who had been waiting impatiently, came out the house and the happy reunion started. I had been waiting a long time for this moment. I had a great love and respect for my grandfather. He had emigrated to America in 1906 and, with great sacrifice, had been able to create a solid financial base for his family. For many years he had crossed the ocean to go to see wife and children and every time would bring his savings to buy a parcel of land or an apartment to provide financial support and security for them. He had also saved enough to buy the two apartment buildings here and the one-family house where he was living with my grand-mother, two uncles, and Aunt Flora.

Here I was now, in front of that mythical figure I had missed during my childhood. My relatives had talked often about him; my mother, who practically grew up without a father, always re-minded us about *Nonno* who was in America working and sacri-ficing for us all. As a child, I missed sitting on his lap reading a book, or listening to him tell a story: I discovered only later that he was an incredible storyteller. He was always present in my mind as a mythical figure; in my imaginary world I would see him building railroads in the open fields of the West, or working in factories, enveloped by the smoke of the roaring machines. His picture in my grandmother's living room in Italy had helped me to see him and keep him in my memory. When I came to America and learned more about his past, I realized that my fantasy had kept me very close to my real *nonno*. When I read his autobiog-raphy many years later, I was moved at discovering how tough his life had been and how big he truly was.

The America that welcomed my *nonno* was very different than the one I was finding. It was an America much less tolerant, with much prejudice against Italians and with very few safety nets. My grandfather and the immigrants of his generation came to an America when many businessmen and industrialists (often called "robber barons") made their fortunes in a nation of unregulated capitalism and labor that created high occupational health risks and exploitation. Union and labor rights were virtually nonexistent, and working conditions were often horrendous. In the textile factories where my grandfather was employed for a while, workers started at the age of fourteen, and many died before the age of twenty-five due to accidents and unhealthy work conditions. My grandfather and many of his compatriots were smart enough to get involved in the labor unions to fight for some protections. However, after the 1917 Bolshevik Revolution, concerns about radicalism were so great that the Red Scare drove xenophobia and racial intolerance to high levels. Pervasive suspicion was directed toward leaders of the American labor movement, many of whom were Italians. Consequently, in addition to being viewed as different from, as well as inferior to, the Anglo-Saxon race that comprised the American majority and being stereotyped as common criminals, Italians were also branded as violent radicals involved in illegal and subversive activities. In addition to the stigma of the Mafia, Italian immigrants had to carry the stereotype of political radicals who were, in turn, linked to crime. Americans feared that Italian immigrant radicals would try to bring down the American government or damage American business. Although it is true that many Italian Americans were part of the emerging labor movement in the early twentieth century, it is inaccurate to say that all Italian immigrants and labor union organizers were radicals who used violence as a tactic. To succeed in this kind of environment, my grandfather and his *paesani* had to work much harder than other national groups and be very honest. World War II further set back the cause of Italian acceptance into American society because one of America's enemies in the war was Italy. Suspicion against Italian immigrants and Italian Americans was strong enough during the war that many Italian American families were forced by U.S. government officials to relocate from the California coast for fear that they might have assisted Italian enemy infiltrators. Some Italians were even put into internment camps for the duration of the war. Even after the war, for many decades Italian Americans experienced both subtle and blatant forms of prejudice, including having to endure insults about their ethnicity.

Having my grandfather before me, I had that piece of history flashing in my mind. *Nonno*, as most of the emigrants of his generation, had done many kinds of labor. My grandfather had worked in the open fields of Pennsylvania building railroad tracks, had been in the factories of New York making rugs, and taking care of the homes of wealthy people in Westchester County as a landscaper. As with most of his compatriots, his uprooting had been caused by economic rather than political or religious motivations. But in order to emigrate, those people also needed guts, a sense of adventure, and an innate Ulysses-like desire for discovery; that is why not all poor people emigrate. The story of Italian immigration is both one of courage, faith, and dignity and of shipwrecks, exploitation, child labor, lynchings, and crowded tenements. I could not separate my grandfather from that (hi)story. And I say this not to solicit pity for him and millions like him, but to solicit admiration. He had come to America at age sixteen to make money and then go back. Unlike Jews fleeing pogroms or African slaves, most Italians chose to leave their homeland legally and therefore always had the option to return. Thus, my grandfather returned many times and many times came back leaving behind his growing family. Living in America by himself he could work intensely and maximize his savings; and he did both. America needed large numbers of sturdy laborers for heavy construction work, and Italian emigrants, my grandfather included, played a key role in building America, for they dug the ditches, toiled in the mines, laid the rails, and carried the bricks and mortar. They gave their sweat and blood to lay the material foundation of America. I am still amazed today at how much those people were able to accomplish while facing huge obstacles and enduring terrible hardship. Through hard work and perseverance they overcame great barriers to prosper in every sector of American life. Their children, as leaders in business, academia, and public service, and as members of our armed forces, have played a pivotal role in shaping the character of this country and driving the progress of the Union. It is above all for these reasons that I consider my *nonno* and the immigrants of his generation our indisputable heroes.

The remembrances of my grandfather are filtered through the

lenses that I have as a grandfather myself living that experience with the memories of a childhood spent without a grandfather. My paternal grandfather had already died before I was born and lived only through a picture in my parents' bedroom and by the story my mother had told us. My father never talked about his father; it was more out of a sense of *riservatezza* rather than lack of care for his father. As a grandfather now, I am living to the fullest the experience that my paternal grandfather missed due to his premature death and that my maternal grandfather missed living far away as an emigrant. I am enjoying this moment. I did not have the opportunity to be as good a father as I would have liked because of the immigrant mission and determination to succeed through hard work, but grandfatherhood is giving me a second chance to look back and to try to "do it better": Work, although still important today, comes second. It is also more fun. Since I do not have the direct responsibility of raising my grandchildren toward the desired goal of life, love for them is not as burdened by doubts and anxieties as it was when my own children were growing up. Relieved of the immediate stresses and the responsibilities of fatherhood, we grandparents may enjoy our grandchildren more than I enjoyed my own children. Because my children are grown, everything seems to be taking care of itself and no one really needs me. Having grandchildren gives me the chance to teach, give advice, tell stories, be a financial and emotional resource, and contribute to their lives. As a result, I still feel valuable. It's that "second lease on life" you always hear people talk about.

The presence of grandchildren makes us lighten up a little. Time is short at this stage of life, and it's just not worth the energy to demand perfection from everyone, especially young children. It also gives us the chance to shamelessly spoil someone without being accused of being a bad father. Grandparenthood is also a time of payback. Remember all those times when your kid told you how much she hated you and how she would never, never, ever be as horrible a parent as you were? Well, chances are that now that they are parents, my children have become a lot more sympathetic to the errors I made when I was the dad and they were the kids. The presence of grandchildren brings back the past.

Grandparents get to relive the memories of the early phase of their own parenthood in observing the growth and development of their grandchildren. Grandparenthood may also bring back some memories of our relationship with our own grandparents. And while I play with my grandchildren I am wondering if my younger brothers and sisters were able to provide to my grandfather some of the joy he had missed in his earlier years. No question, the memories of my encounter with my grandfather are shaping my behavior as a grandfather. He is a reminder that we enjoy today the fruits of investments that were made by our parents and grandparents. If we don't invest in our children just as they did, then our grandchildren will not have the benefits nor the standard of living we enjoy today.

Because of the investments my grandparents made in the future, our arrival in America as immigrants had none of the insecurity and humiliating conditions found by my grandfather. No question that every immigrant goes through a traumatic experience because of the many living adjustments that must be made, but the degree or level of those adjustments may be very different from era to era and from situation to situation. As the eight of us got out of the cars at 242nd Street in the Bronx, we found ourselves standing in front of the buildings owned by my grandfather. More reassuring, waiting for us there were many close relatives who had achieved and were achieving higher education.

In fact, as we arrived, my Aunt Elvira and my cousins came down from the apartment building to embrace us. The strangeness of the new environment was mitigated by the joy of seeing our cousins. They had arrived six years earlier because they had been found "politically clean." They had arrived in America in 1954, less than a year after my grandparents filed the immigration papers. They were living in one of my grandfather's apartments and had settled well in the new culture. The seven Lonardo children already spoke fluent English and were all going to school; the older ones — Gianni, Pinuccio, Pupa, and Marisa were working while going to school at night; the younger three — Rosalba, Guido, and Agnese — were in secondary and elementary schools. Thanks to them, to their generous efforts and love, our shock with the new culture was not as traumatic. We became very close and have remained close. While we were getting reacquainted, my Uncle Gaetano, realizing that it would have helped to socialize with a refreshment or something to eat, asked me to go with him to buy some ice cream. We got in the car and left.

My attention turned to the fire escapes on the buildings, a novelty for us. When I expressed my puzzlement, my uncle said, "America is different and learn how to appreciate the differences." I could not digest those ugly metal fire escapes right in front of the buildings and I told him so, "I understand that the construction here is different, that there are other necessities, but that doesn't mean that things cannot be beautiful." It was my first clash with the American sense of aesthetic; it persisted through the years. We continued the short ride without talking. When we arrived at the store, Carvel, Uncle Guy proceeded with the order: "A gallon of strawberry and lemon." What a shock; in America ice cream came in gallons. We were used buying, on special occasions, a cup or a cone, usually the smallest ones, and here it was in gallons. Wow, once more America is the land of abundance, I thought.

On the way home, the huge electrical poles with so many wires hanging along the street puzzled me. It was such an ugly sight that a remark escaped from me: "Why do they have all these wires hanging; why don't they bury them underground?" My uncle could not believe that I was focusing only on the aesthetic and not on the practicality of things or on the abundance that Americans enjoyed. He snapped back, "You are coming from a house without electricity, telephone, gas, water, and sewer, and you complain about the look of the fire escapes and the utility wires hanging along the street? What's matter with you? Think about what we have and the difference it makes in our lives." I was happy to be back home to get out of the embarrassment. We went inside and celebrated our arrival with the big gallons of ice cream.

As we were eating the ice cream I quickly realized that it was different from the gelato I occasionally had enjoyed in Italy: It was the consistency, temperature, and the taste. I did not dare to make any comments, especially because all my "American" relatives were commenting how good it was. Even after so many years, I have never been able to appreciate American ice cream over gelato. I learned through the years that the two delicacies are different. Gelato is made with milk, not cream, and it contains 2 percent-8 percent fat depending on the folded-in ingredients, while American ice cream contains more fat, ranging from 16 percent to 30 percent. Also, gelato is churned at a slower speed than ice cream, so it's denser because not as much air is whipped into the mixture. As a result, gelato contains about 25 to 30 percent air, while ice cream can contain as much as 50 percent air. Finally, while ice cream is typically served frozen, gelato is typically stored and served at a slightly warmer temperature, so it's not quite completely frozen. The overly cold American ice cream freezes the pores on the tongue on the first mouthful and prevents the full enjoyment of flavors, while the gelato with not as much fat doesn't coat the mouth in the same way, so the flavors are more intense. I didn't know all this when I ate the first ice cream, but even if I had known it, I would not have dared to make any comments on a day when we were celebrating our arrival in America and long-awaited family reunion.

The family reunion was proceeding remarkably well. I quickly connected with my cousin Gianni. He was four years older, but at our age that difference didn't mean anything. We chatted and laughed the whole afternoon. My sisters connected with their female cousins, and my younger brothers did the same with my younger male cousins. The Lonardo cousins, being the same ages as we, were a blessing to us; they became our bridge to American culture and life. They introduced us to everything. They had a car and with them we learned the streets of the Bronx, Manhattan, and Westchester. Because we were not able to afford a car for three years, they helped us when walking and mass transit could not meet our needs.

My grandparents' home was not big; in fact, the rooms were very small. They were much smaller than the rooms of our house in Italy. The dozen and a half relatives could barely move in the dining and living rooms. I was amazed by the construction in wood and by the low ceiling; I felt so closed in. I dared to express my surprise to Gianni. Calmly he said, "The construction in heavy timber with lighter components is like Ford's idea for cars, it facilitates production, keeps the cost low, and makes the product accessible to more Americans. Yes, these wooden houses are flimsy by Italian standards. They are more vulnerable to fire, have higher maintenance, and are part of the American Kleenex culture in being relatively ephemeral." My lord, the American greatness was evaporating right in front of my eyes. Italian houses were obviously built to last generations. The Mignone house, in which Uncle Agostino was living, had chiseled into the stone, at the front entrance, "*Proprietà Mignone*" and had belonged to the Mignones for four hundred years. These matchboxes, I thought, will not even last for one generation.

I could not understand why I was so disappointed and was being so critical. I had left a house without running water, heat, electricity, sewer, and telephone and was now complaining about aesthetic, size, and longevity.

When it was time to settle in, *Nonno* took us to our apartment next door. It was a one-bedroom apartment with a living room, small eat-in-kitchen, and a bathroom. It was difficult to fit eight people. My grandmother suggested that the two older girls, Matilde and Maria, should live in their house; Mamma, the boys, little Agnese, and I would settle in the apartment. We were cramped, but we found a way to make it work.

Jet lag was pulling us down. We had left Benevento the morning of the day before, almost forty hours ago, and exhaustion was taking its toll. Agnese was cranky; Domenico had fallen asleep on the sofa. Nino and Biagio were still trying to figure out how we were going to sleep.

Finally in bed, I was tossing and turning. It was not just the new bed that was giving me problems. I was concerned about how we were going to move on with our lives. *Nonno* would not mind feeding us for a few days, but we needed to establish our independence. How were we going to realize our American Dream? Gianni had told me during our long chat that the best way to handle things was to try to turn any situation into something great. "Have a positive attitude at all times. This is our life; let's work hard and let's enjoy it. America puts the world at our fingertips.

It's all up to us. And if sometimes you don't get what you want, it may be a *colpo* of luck." It sounded good, but those words were also creating anxiety.

Thinking about how I was going to step out of the house and begin my new life was not a comforting way to go to sleep. So, instead, I started to think about the girls I was going to possibly meet. In Italy we had the impression that American girls were easy to take to bed. With that thought I slowly fell into a deep sleep and had a wonderful dream. I was back in Italy and I had met an American girl with whom I had some magical moments. I was with a blonde American in my hometown, which looked like something out of a storybook. I invited her for an espresso and then for a long walk on some historic streets explaining to her the whole history of the city—whom the fountains are named after, whom the statues represented. She was listening and the whole time I was looking deep into her eyes as though she were the only woman on the entire planet. At a certain point I said that I loved my homeland even more now that I had seen it through her eyes. She kissed me and I was lost in oblivion.

During the next couple of days, we met new people, some of whom became good friends for the rest of our lives. One of them was Rocco Pallone, my future brother-in-law. Rocco was one of Gianni's best friends: He was enrolled at City College with Gianni and lived very close by. He became a permanent fixture around the house: At night and on the weekend he would come over and just hang out. Naturally we were very happy to see him because we had a lot in common. Although he was not from Benevento but from Roccasecca, south of Rome, we practically shared the same dialect and came from the same social milieu.

The presence of Rocco, in addition to my cousin Gianni, made my encounter with America a relatively easy transition. Rocco, a man of few words, was very enigmatic. When Gianni would talk and inform me about American life, Rocco would only make brief explicative comments of five, seven words. I learned from their conversation how Italians were still discriminated against, perceived as criminals, and viewed with suspicion. World War II had further set back the cause of Italian acceptance into American society because Italy was one of America's enemies, and the last few years of the Fascist regime had done a lot of damage to the Italian image. Even though I had grown up facing constant prejudice or facing rejection by my classmates for being the son of a farmer when I went to school in the city, this new form of possible prejudice in a completely unknown environment was creating anxiety.

THREE

We came to America at a truly special time. America and the Western world were embarking on an anthropological revolution that brought about profound economic, social, political, and cultural transformation. Even from Italy we could sense the tide of change. During that summer, the 1960 Italian Olympic Games had already offered the dawn of a new era. The Games became the athletic epitome of the cheerful era that the world was about to experience. The athletes were opening up a new trend. In the newly constructed "Palazzo dello Sport" that hosted the Olympic boxing event, an eighteen-year-old African-American athlete won the gold medal and began his own revolution prior to becoming a "King"; he began a career in which he became a legendary figure known around the world. He was Cassius Clay. In the same games, in the track and field events at the "Olympia," the star was the African-American athlete Wilma Rudolf. Her nickname "Gazelle" justified her success in the three gold medals earned in 100m, 200m and 4X100m races.

Without knowing it, the Olympic games in Rome were telling us a lot. We were at the beginning of a decade of social turmoil and profound cultural changes. Everything was starting to be questioned, especially "the establishment": race relations, sexual mores, women's rights, traditional modes of authority, experimentation with psychedelics and marijuana, and interpretations of the American Dream regarding consumerism. New cultural forms emerged, including the pop music of four young British boys, The Beatles, which rapidly evolved to shape and reflect the emphasis on change and experimentation of the youth culture. Additional musical groups from the United Kingdom as well as a growing number of topical American singers and songwriters also impacted the counterculture movement. The youth generation, sucked in by the current, wanted to be free but also to give freedom.

The need to address minority rights of women, the handicapped, and many other neglected constituencies within the larger population came to the forefront as an increasing number of primarily younger people broke free from the constraints of 1950s orthodoxy in a desire to create a more inclusive and tolerant social landscape.

When we arrived in America we could feel the air of novelty and changes. Prosperity, educational opportunities, social transformations were breaking the rigid walls of class stratifications and racial barriers. Americans looked toward the future with sheer optimism.

My siblings and I, along with all the other new immigrants, were engulfed by this wind of transformation. America was opening herself up to us with a benevolent heart. So often we would say, "What a country! God bless America." Two months after we had arrived in America, John F. Kennedy was elected President. Kennedy, the first and only Catholic and the first Irish American President, the only President to have won a Pulitzer Prize. At his inaugural address on January 20th, 1961, Kennedy challenged the people of the United States with the statement: "Ask not what your country can do for you, but rather what you can do for your country" and wanted the young people of the country to help the undeveloped world. He announced the establishment of the Peace Corps, a program that intended to send 10,000 young volunteers to serve in Africa, Asia, and Latin America and to help in areas such as education, farming, health care, and construction.

It was a new era also for *Italianità*. On the radio, Italian American singers were dominating the magnetic waves. As one turned the knob of station after station, the melodious voices of Italian American singers were reverberating in the air with love songs, very often with Italian words. Perry Como, Tony Bennett, Frank Sinatra, Dean Martin, Julius La Rosa, Louie Prima, Frankie Avalon, Bobby Darin, Vic Damone, Nicola Pericoli, Dion were entertaining the wide American audience with "Beyond the Sea," "I Love You Because," "*Al di là*," "Night and Day," "It's Impossible," "That's *Amore*," "Return to Me," "*Cara Mia*," "*Buona sera*," "You Light up my Life." 1960 was the year when *Where the Boys Are* was released, which revolved around a group of college women spending spring break at the beach in Fort Lauderdale. The title song "Where the Boys Are" was sung by an Italian American star Concetta Rosa Maria Franconero, known professionally as Connie Francis. *Where the Boys Are* was one of the first teen films to explore adolescent sexuality and the changing sexual mores and attitudes among American college youth. It started a process that completely changed sexuality to this day. It was the first movie that I saw in America. My cousin Gianni, along with a couple of his friends, took me out and, although I could barely make sense of the language spoken on the screen, I was fully taken in by the American youth energy. That youth and energy was later given powerful expression by the blooming Italian American star John Travolta as Tony Manero in *Saturday Night Fever* (1977) and as Danny Zucco in *Grease* (1978). America appeared so full of life and offered so much hope. "What a country!" I would say to myself. My brothers and sisters, probably too young to understand what was happening, were finding pleasure in the new cultural and social environment.

In the early sixties, pizza had not yet replaced hot dogs as the most popular American food, Starbucks had not yet invaded the world with its *"espresso"* and *"cappuccino grande,"* wine enjoyment was practically an ethnic or elite drink, Wonder Bread was the most popular sandwich bread, and Italian restaurants were still confined to Italian neighborhoods mostly catering to Italian Americans... but not for too much longer. The walls of ethnicity were breaking down and assimilation was increasingly giving in to integration and a different kind of acculturation.

We arrived in America when the emerging youth subculture was steadily increasing its impact on the rest of society through its tastes in fashion, music, and consumer culture. Education, in particular, was among the factors that accounted for the gradual and inexorable rise of Italian Americans in American society. Moreover, with the improved economic status of second and third generations, the ties of the Italian family began to loosen enough to accommodate greater individual ambitions. While education was almost anathema to the first generation, second- and third-generation Italian Americans gradually became almost obsessive in seeking a quality education for their children. This attitude has had a dramatic impact on the number of college-educated Italian Americans. In 1964 America was opening on the average a college per week, and new social classes were entering the walls of academia. Italian Americans, too, were sucked in by the anthropological revolution.

In the reawakening of racial and ethnic identities, Italians played a role in the Civil Rights Movement. I remember the prominence of Monsignor Geno C. Baroni (1930-1984). While assigned as pastor from 1960 to1965 in the Washington, D.C., parish of Sts. Paul and Augustine, a merger of white and black parishes, applying the Catholic social doctrine in ministering to urban poor, his dedication to civil rights propelled him into a national leadership role. In March 1963 he was coordinator for Martin Luther King's March on Washington; and in 1964 he went to Mississippi and marched in the 1965 Selma civil rights demonstrations. His work was complemented by another priest, James E. Groppi (1930-1985), who in 1963 also took a leading role in the civil rights march on Washington going the following year to Selma, Alabama, to support King. Unlike King, he advocated direct and violent response. The struggle for civil rights was also a struggle for human rights and a fight against all forms of oppression and discrimination. Italian Americans, too, were vindicating their ethnic identity with pride.

We arrived when Italian Americans were shaking from their shoulders the heavy burden of prejudice and claiming back their self-esteem. The high volume of sales of *The Italians*, by Luigi Barzini (1908-1984) in 1964 was another strong sign that Italian Americans were eagerly interested in the recovery of their cultural roots. They purchased and read with great interest a book that delved deeply into the Italian national character and presented, not always with the favorable predisposition of the reader, both its great qualities and its imperfections. The image of an Italy in the grips of the "economic miracle" and a society interested in embodying the life of spectacle reflected in the movies of Fellini, Antonioni, Visconti, Pasolini, and so many other directors, which were shown on American screens, certainly provided new energy to the desire to reconnect with the ancestral land.

At the same time, the sixties were years of excitement and hope for Italian artistic culture as well. Design culture moved rapidly from design for artisans to design for industry, that is, to "industrial design." The profound cultural and social changes of the period provided the impetus for the nation to enter the even more turbulent seas of international competition. This is particularly visible in the flourishing of Italian movies, which became extremely popular both at home and abroad. Fellini made *La Dolce Vita* (1960). Marcello Mastroianni and Sophia Loren became international stars. Antonioni, Fellini, Pasolini, Bertolucci, the Taviani brothers, and Scola all became famous as filmmakers.

Self-discovery was taking place by building a bridge between the past and the present of the "old country" with the cultural and social environment of the American landscape. After the publication of *The Africans* (1967), by Harold Courtlander, but before *Roots* (1976), by Alex Haley, which with its huge popularity increased interest in genealogy and ethnic identity, Richard Gambino's *Blood of My Blood: The Dilemma of the Italian Americans* (1974) offered to many Italian Americans a voyage of discovery into their ethnic identity. Gambino's best-selling exploration of the psychological impact of the ethnic identity of America's Italians was another clear indication of the blossoming self-confidence of Italian Americans in their ethnicity. In the same year a pioneer work in the field of Italian American Studies appeared on the American literary scene: *The Italian-American Novel* (1974), by Rose Basile Green. This systematization by an Italian American scholar of narrative written by Italian American writers in a critical cultural and literary context gave yet another stimulus to the desire to assess and expose the American *Italianità*. The creation of the American Italian Historical Association (AIHA) in 1966 to systematically and scientifically assess Italian American experience and to launch Italian American Studies pulled together a network of dedicated scholars from various disciplines. Its first multidisciplinary conference, held in New York City at the Casa Italiana of Columbia University on October 26, 1968, put into motion a process that through the years has constructed the history and the story of the Italian American Experience in a deeper and broader way than that presented by Hollywood. And in 1975, a coalition of business, political, educational, labor, and community leaders organized the National Italian American Foundation (NIAF) to promote Italian American culture and heritage through lectures, symposia, conferences, scholarships, fellowships, and scholarly and community cultural grants.

We had left Italy when there was the supposed economic miracle, but thousands of Southern Italians were migrating to the North or emigrating abroad. Unquestionably the economic reconstruction had taken off and within twenty years would place Italy among the world's top six economic powers. The center-left government introduced profound changes, including the nationalization of some services, democratization of the education system, and the beginning of the "welfare state." Eventually, these changes also affected the South, the villages and the lands from which for decades people had been forced to find a better life elsewhere. And while that was beginning to take place, we had been pulled by the current of that river of human flesh flowing toward the sea of hope and dreams.

We came to America when mass education and social affluence gave rise to an unprecedented influence of young people. The emerging youth subculture steadily increased its impact on the rest of society, and through its tastes in fashion, music, and consumer culture, helped create a mood of novelty and changes. Although youth subculture was not monolithic, it created a vast new market of its own in the merchandise of popular culture.

The introduction of new technology — television (including Telstar), long-playing phonograph records, transistor radios, modernized telephone systems, jet travel, labor-saving products such as refrigerators and washing-machines, the contraceptive pill — helped to advance the anthropological revolution. The advent of television, providing unprecedented international cultural influence, played a leading role in social transformation. Massive improvements in material life, so that large sections of society joined the consumer society — which in backward areas of Italy meant the arrival of electricity, together with inside running water — moved many people at the fringe of society into the "civilized world." My siblings and I, with all the other immigrants, were engulfed by this wind of transformation. America was opening up to us with a benevolent heart. And very often we would respond, "What a country! God bless America."

After John F. Kennedy was assassinated and Lyndon B. Johnson took over, the flow of changes continued at an even higher speed. The "Great Society" legislation that included laws that upheld civil rights, Public Broadcasting, Medicare, Medicaid, environmental protection, aid to education, and the War on Poverty had a profound impact on the whole of American society, and my generation was feeling the energy of transformation most profoundly.

Johnson's belief that education could cure both ignorance and poverty became an essential component of the American Dream, especially for minorities, and became a top priority of the Great Society, with an emphasis on helping poor children. After the 1964 landslide brought in many new liberal congressmen, for the first time the President had enough votes for the Elementary and Secondary Education Act (ESEA) of 1965 to enable large amounts of federal money to go to public schools. In practice ESEA meant helping all public-school districts with more money going to districts that had large proportions of students from poor families (this included all big cities). Johnson's second major education program was the Higher Education Act of 1965, which focused on funding for lower-income students including grants, work-study money, and government loans. He set up the National Endowment for the Humanities and the National Endowment for the Arts. In 1967 Johnson signed the Public Broadcasting Act to create educational television programs to supplement the broadcast networks. Years later, I benefitted from the federal benevolence for education: I received full financial support for three years with an NDEA Title IV (National Defense Education Act) to pursue my PhD. "What a country!"

The African American civil rights movement was part of this profound social and cultural transformation. The movement exploded in major riots in black neighborhoods in a series of "long hot summers." They started with a violent disturbance in Harlem in 1964 and the Watts district of Los Angeles in 1965 and extending to 1970. The biggest wave came in April 1968, when riots occurred in over a hundred cities in the wake of the assassination of Martin Luther King. Newark burned in 1967, where six days of rioting left 26 dead, 1,500 injured, and the inner city a burned-out shell. In Detroit in 1967, Governor George Romney sent in 7,400 National Guard troops to quell fire bombings, looting, and attacks on businesses and police. Finally Johnson sent in federal troops with tanks and machine guns. Detroit continued to burn for three more days until finally 43 were dead, 2,250 were injured and 4,000 were arrested; property damage ranged into the hundreds of millions of dollars; much of inner Detroit was never rebuilt. Johnson called for even more billions to be spent in the cities and on another federal civil rights law regarding housing, but his political capital had been spent, and his Great Society programs lost support. Johnson's popularity plummeted as a massive white political backlash took shape, reinforcing the sense that Johnson had lost control of the streets of major cities as well of as his party. However, a dominant principle was taking root: that men and women from all backgrounds have common beliefs and aspirations, common rights, and a common responsibility in relationship with each other.

The economic landscape was populated by people who had great respect for the state and its citizens and still cared about the common good. Wall Street did not dominate the economic and political scene. There wasn't the greed, hubris, and incompetence that ruined it later. We miss that era when we think about today's reckless borrowing and risk taking, creative accounting, political connections, fragmented oversight, the cavalier attitude toward customers, and excessive compensation for chief executives.

In retrospect, looking back to that time, America was truly great. People had full confidence in the American capitalist system. No screaming of "American greed!" The average American felt that the economic system was fair and offered many opportunities. In those years, no one would have imagined that people lived under a vulture capitalism that operated exclusively for the benefit of blood-sucking CEOs. Issues such as massive debt and overreaching government, fairness and inequality were not part of dinnertime discussion in our still cohesive family unit. We knew that Mr. Rockefeller was very rich and that there were many more Americans rich like him, but the average American did not feel hatred toward them. People were not looking for a government, a political party, a Congress that would stand up to the greedy rich who pillaged the 99 percent and robbed the middle class of hope. People were not castigating political leaders, political parties, and a judicial system for protecting and enabling the plutocrats, the exploiters who had profited while America suffered. Middle-class America was not angry because politicians put their party over people and political power over everything. No one felt suffocated in a system where the rich use money to exercise disproportionate political influence. No one felt the angst of leaving to his or her children a republic that is rotten at the core.

It certainly concerns me where we are presently. I believe that my brothers and sisters feel the same way. We've worked hard since we were children. We still put in fifty-hour weeks and call in sick only when really sick. We all have made reasonable salaries, but we didn't inherit our jobs or our income, and we worked to get where we are. Thus, not to be misjudged by what I said before, it upsets me to hear that we must "spread our wealth" to people who don't share our work ethic; that we must do it as a simple humanitarian responsibility. It upsets me to hear that the government will take the money we earned, by force if necessary, and give it to people too lazy or unambitious to earn it. It upsets me to hear people, rich and poor, claiming entitlements.

It upsets me to hear that, out of "tolerance for other cultures," we must let Saudi Arabia and other Arab countries use our oil money to fund mosques and madrassa Islamic schools to preach hate in Australia, New Zealand, the U.K., America, and Canada, while no one from these countries is allowed to fund a church, synagogue, or religious school in Saudi Arabia or any other Arab country to teach love and tolerance. It upsets me to hear that we must lower our living standard to fight global warming, which no one is allowed to debate.

It upsets me to hear that drug addicts have a disease and we must help support and treat them and pay for the damage they do. Did a giant germ rush out of a dark alley, grab them, and stuff white powder up their noses or stick a needle in their arm while they tried to fight it off?

It upsets me to hear wealthy athletes, entertainers, and politicians of all parties talking about innocent mistakes, stupid mistakes, or youthful mistakes when we all know they think their only mistake was getting caught.

It really upsets me to hear people who don't take responsibility for their lives and actions. It tires me to hear them blame the government or discrimination or big whatever for their problems.

It also really upsets me to see young men and women in their teens and early twenties bedeck themselves in tattoos and face studs, thereby making themselves unemployable and then claiming money from the government.

Some of us are happy to enter our mature age mostly because we will not have to see the world these people are making. I personally feel sorry for my grandchildren and their children because they are going to live in this kind of world and they will not have experienced the world of the 1960s.

When we came to America we wanted to quickly become part of the American cultural texture and were very respectful of the symbols and codes that incarnated the American national unity. Although we supported social changes and respect for ethical values, we never showed any disdain for the principles on which the country was founded. Consequently, it always upset us to hear people malign America. You can imagine how we would feel in later years when some "Americans," worrying about whether we were offending some individual or their culture, would permit an attack on our basic principles and historical cultural identity. This culture has been developed over two centuries of struggles, trials, and victories by millions of men and women who have sought freedom. Most Americans believe in a God who is not some Christian, right wing, political preacher. God is part of our American culture. Our motto should be this: 'This is OUR COUNTRY, OUR LAND, and OUR LIFESTYLE, and we will allow you every opportunity to enjoy it all. However, once you are done complaining, whining, and griping about Our Flag, Our Pledge, Our Religious Beliefs, or Our Way of Life, I highly encourage you take advantage of one other great American freedom, 'THE RIGHT TO LEAVE.'

Since I arrived in this country, I have been of the firm belief that if one isn't happy here then LEAVE. No one is forced to come here. However, when one decides to come, he/she must accept the country. Immigrants, not Americans, must adapt. You asked to be here. So accept the country YOU sought. "We will accept your beliefs, and will not question why. All we ask is that you accept ours and live in harmony and peaceful enjoyment with us."

It is especially for these reasons that I cherish the 1960s: We wanted to succeed by becoming part of the nation that had accepted us rather than fighting against it to impose our values. In that incredible period of profound social and cultural transformation of the country, those of us who had just arrived here were astonished by the social and cultural flow and energized by it. We were taken along, and I don't know who was changing faster and more profoundly, the nation or us. My family had come from an agrarian society where life had remained still for centuries; the only change experienced was that caused by the movement of seasons. In America, we knew that uprooting was going to require many adjustments, but we had arrived when America was at the beginning of an anthropological revolution, and we were being transported by the current, by an unparalleled social and cultural surge.

For us the challenge was to adjust to the American way of life. Americans were people who ate peanut butter and jelly sandwiches on mushy white bread. I tried to imitate them a few times. I asked my mother to buy Wonder Bread for sandwiches so that when I ate them in the factory I was one of them at least in eating. But I just did not know how to handle that bread that would stick under my palate. I tried smaller bites and different fillings, but to no avail. America was eating a terrible bread, and I quickly gave it up. And America did the same: today one has to search hard to find that sticky, gluey tasteless bread.

Our habits and traditions could never be purely American. Thanksgiving and Christmas tables were not set with just turkey and stuffing, potatoes and cranberry sauce. We had turkey but only after antipasto, soup, lasagna, meatballs, and salad with several side dishes ending with fruit, nuts, pastries, and homemade cookies with colored sprinkles.

FOUR

We spent the first few days in the Bronx getting acquainted with the area and meeting people. My cousins played hosts. Each of them took one of us under his wings. I had hooked up with Gianni and drove around with him, mostly in Mount Vernon, the city in which we eventually did our business and worked. In the evening some of my cousins' friends came over, most of them Italian immigrants who had arrived within the last five, eight years. Because we did not speak English, my cousins tried to connect us with as many people as possible who spoke Italian. On the second day at our new home, *Nonna*, Uncle Vincent, and Aunt Flora arrived from Italy, which they had visited during the Olympics. They saw only a couple of events, but had succeeded in dealing with the American Consulate on our behalf. They obtained the visa for us and waited to come back to America until they made sure that we had left for the U.S.

Since we arrived in early September, schools were already in session and my siblings needed to be enrolled. The same day *Zia* Flora arrived from Italy, she took my brothers to schools and registered them. Nino, almost thirteen, was enrolled in John Phillip Sousa Junior High School; Biagio and Domenico, respectively ten and eight, were enrolled in an elementary school, PS 16. Maria, fifteen, became a student at Evanderchild High School. Matilde and I, respectively eighteen and twenty, were old enough to work; therefore, school had to be limited to night classes at Roosevelt High School to learn English. Agnese, age four, stayed home with my mother.

It was a confusing beginning for all of us because the kids were enrolled in schools without any guidance and the schools were not yet socially opened. Biagio, despite being two years older than Domenico, was placed in third grade; Domenico instead in fifth. Domenico came home crying because he could not understand anything; while Biagio, on the other hand, complained that the math was too easy. After some juggling, they were assigned to the correct classes. In those years there were no ESL courses. Immigrants, while not knowing a word of English, would be thrown into regular classes: It was full immersion, American style! Anyone can imagine the shock and frustration of my brothers and all the immigrant children with no knowledge of English sitting in a regular class with American students who spoke only English. It was a slow and systematic process. In those first few weeks, the learning process was limited to copying down in notebooks whatever was written on the board and making some sense of it. Somehow it worked: When Domenico reached high school he became the editor of the student newspaper! In a matter of four years, he had achieved a knowledge of English that was better than the average of his peers.

The one-bedroom apartment that *Nonno* had prepared for us had been furnished with various pieces of furniture that he had been able to get from friends and tenants in his buildings. Although the space was not large enough to accommodate eight people, it was warm and neat. With the splitting of my siblings between our apartment and my grandparents' house, we were managing. Certainly, it was not an ideal setting or what we expected in America. In fact, coming to America, the living space had decreased and, frankly, we were disappointed. But how could we have complained after all that *Nonno* and the rest of the family had sacrificed in order to prepare for the arrival of eight family members at once?

My grandparents not only provided us with shelter, but were also providing us with food and every other need. In reality, they had to have true love, courage, and determination to take on such a large family with so many young children. A family of eight people with the prospect of only two able to work! They needed more than love and courage to assume the responsibility to feed eight mouths for an undetermined amount of time. The emigrant experience and faith in the job market sustained their determination.

Although our American family was extremely happy that we had finally joined them and did not mind the heavy sacrifice to support us, we did not want to become a burden anymore than necessary. I was anxious to start to work to earn the money that eventually would lessen our burden on them and would also start to give us some independence. And I was ready and willing to do any type of work. Clearly, I did not have a choice. Could I spend days looking for the job that I liked or that fulfilled my aspirations? I was and had to be ready for anything as long as I was able to bring home a paycheck.

Four days after our arrival, *Zia* Flora took on the task of taking me around looking for a job. It was not an easy undertaking but she had the right personality for it. We got in the car and went to Mount Vernon. "On Fourth Avenue there are several factories and I am sure that in one of them I should be able to find you a job," she said with an assuring tone. After a ten-minute drive we parked the car and started the search. Not knowing any English, I depended completely on her skills of introduction. I knew that she was very convincing when she talked, so that gave me some confidence. Like a little pet I followed her. It was a strange feeling to be pulled around like that because I had grown up doing things on my own; as the second of eight children, I had to learn at an early age to do things by myself. I had to grow up fast: It was a healthy process, however, because when I made mistakes I was young enough to learn and to avoid making them in the mature years of my life. However, in this new situation, without knowing the language, here I was, like a little dog, following my aunt. She opened the entrance door of the first factory and with confidence spoke to the lady at the reception desk. After two or three minutes, which to me felt like ten or fifteen, she turned to me and said, "There are no openings, not even to clean the shop." "Don't worry," she added, "we will find something." And we moved to the next building.

We entered and she proceeded in the same imploring tone. She must have said something like this: "I wonder if you have work for my nephew who just arrived from Italy. He is ready to do anything. He is here with six brothers and sisters and he is the oldest. He needs to find a job immediately so that he can support them. He is a nice young man who is reliable and willing to work hard." From the tone of her voice I could sense that she was pleading on my behalf. She was asked a couple of things; but she did not answer "yes" or "no." Turning to me, back and forth, she was in talking mode to convince and was indicating me as someone capable and enthusiastic about work. But then in a disconcerting tone said, "Let's go, it's a job for which you absolutely have to know how to speak English." We stepped out and we continued what started to seem to me a "via crucis."

I was becoming demoralized; it seemed that we were begging for work. I wanted to work, I needed to work, but it was a bit humiliating to beg or seem desperate. I was wondering if there was an employment office where one could ask for work by just filling an application in which one indicated skills and qualifications. "This is America," I was thinking, "and work should be a sacred right." I felt demoralized and disillusioned: "Here I am, in America, begging to work!"

When we arrived at another factory, we entered and Aunt Flora followed the same routine. She talked for a few minutes. I kept looking at the eyes of the woman at the reception desk to read how the sense of the conversation was going. At a certain point my aunt turned to me and asked, "They want to know if you are available to work ten hours per day. You are able to work ten hours, aren't you?" She was feeding me the answer, but I did not need the bait. "Sure, no problem; that's very good for me," I said in an assertive voice. I did not want to create any doubt and added, "I can work even more hours." To be more convincing, I gave an extra dose, "I will be available to work even on Saturdays, if I am needed." She translated my message and she must have embellished it because the number of words she used was much higher.

Meanwhile, I very intently tried to sense what was going on by reading every facial expression and eye movements in both interlocutors. While the woman was making a call, my aunt turned to me and said, "It seems they have a job opening; she will call the foreman to meet you and he will decide whether or not to offer you the job." I was peeing in my pants. What was he going to ask me? Before I entered the factory I noticed the name of the company; they made some kind of machines. The smell of cut metal indicated that it was a machine tool enterprise.

After we waited a few long minutes, two men came, one cleanly dressed, the other in working clothes. They introduced themselves; George, the foreman, and Hewey the head of one of the departments. Hewey started to talk in a kind of Italian dialect that sounded strange to me. His words were practically these: "So, you would like to work here and are willing to work ten hours a day. I understand that you are also willing to work on Saturdays. That is good because we work half a day almost every Saturday. We start to work at eight o'clock and finish at six-thirty, with a lunch break of half hour at twelve. Is it OK for you?" "Sure, sure, no problem. It's perfect," I said without hesitation and with a convincing voice. "I understand that you have a lot of brothers and sisters and need to work. I will make sure that you get some overtime also on Saturdays. Anything that you work over eight hours every day is overtime and whatever you put in on Saturday is also time and half. *Capisci?*" With some effort I understood everything he was telling me in a mixture of Sicilian and Calabrese dialects. "*Capito, capito,*" I answered, "It's wonderful."

He led me to the area of the factory where I was going to work. It was a drill press located in the middle of the plant. He introduced me to two guys who were working in the area of my future working place. We shook hands smiling and I assumed that they were given the message that I was going to be their companion. There were different departments of machines — lathes, grinding machines, milling machines, radial drill presses, saws, etc. Men were intense at their work. I did not see a single woman. It was clear that it was a men's factory. Walking back to the reception area, he said, "We have health care coverage and paid vacation, but we don't have unions and don't want unions; *capisci?*" "*Capisco,* no problem. I just want to work," I remarked. "By the way, you will get one dollar and twenty cents an hour. I will see you on Monday at eight, *arrivederci.*"

At the reception desk I was given a form to fill out. My aunt wrote everything. I only signed it. The women reviewed it and in a surprised way asked in Italian dialect, "You have indicated four dependents. You are not in Italy anymore; if you lie in America you end up in jail." I did not want to create problems and quickly answered, "I can lower the number, but I will be supporting more than four brothers and sisters. It's no lie." She took the form, gave a sigh, and wished me good luck.

I had been hired by Hertlein Special Tools Co. That was my baptismal water in the American productive system. I was already starting to feel some relief because I could provide some alleviation to my grandparents. I tried to figure out in my mind how much I was going to make per day and per week. Going home, in the car, I looked for a pen or pencil and a piece of paper to do the calculation; I didn't find anything. I forced my mind to keep together hours and dollars; and my calculation indicated that I was going to take home about seventy dollars per week. I did the approximate calculation aloud with my aunt, and again came to be about seventy dollars. My aunt, said cautiously, "There are some deductions for taxes and social security, the pension." "However," she said, "they give you health care; you are covered if you get sick. That's good. Not every worker has health care in America!"

When I got home, my mother greeted us anxiously, but she understood quickly that I had found a job. She had an incredible ability to read the minds and souls of her children. Probably that is why none of us went astray; if we had a problem, before we said anything or if we tried to hide anything, she would ask us how was everything, and if we resisted she would dance around that question until we opened up. "I will start Monday morning and will work until sixty-thirty every day," I said with a big smile. "They also have work on Saturdays until twelve." We went inside our apartment and chatted about the factory and how to prepare for the job.

I needed work clothes. Most of the people at the factory wore light blue pants and shirts. It was almost a standard uniform. However, I was not told to go dressed in any particular attire and therefore did not become concerned if I was unable to conform. But I still needed some working clothes. Uncle Vincent, who wore my same size, gave me a shirt and pants that he used to do work around the house. It was a temporary solution. Once I got the first paycheck, I thought, I would normalize my working identity as a machine tool operator and buy the light blue pants and shirt. My Uncle Vincent also provided me with a pair of working shoes. They weren't very comfortable to stand on for ten hours a day, but they were good enough to use for a few weeks.

My mother was assuming her responsibility of making sure

that I would have everything I needed early in the morning to go to work. "What about lunch and drinks? You will be working for ten hours and are young," she said with concern. "How many sandwiches should I make?" "Ma," I said, "we have two coffee breaks and time for lunch." We figured that I needed something to eat and drink for three times a day. She went next door to my grandparents and figured out what to prepare: one sandwich with cold cuts for the first coffee break, two frittata sandwiches for lunch, and another cold cuts sandwich for the second coffee break. This combination of sandwiches became standard for the approximately four and half years I worked at Hertlein.

"You need a bag to carry your clothes and lunches," said my mother. "You can use the plastic bag that the travel agency gave us in Italy; you can even carry it hanging from your shoulder. You should also be able to fit into it the working clothes." She went into the bedroom and came out with the blue handbag. "Let's check it." She took the working clothes and the shoes and tested the size. It was large enough also for the four sandwiches. "Oh, Madonna, we also need room for something to drink," she said with some angst. We had forgotten that I needed something to drink because we had the habit of not drinking much during the meals; it was a terrible habit that lasted also in our new culture.

Everything was unfamiliar for us. Not only were we dealing with a new culture when we moved to a new country very different from ours, but we were facing a new mode of life. We had moved from an agricultural setting, where we produced the basic food for family needs, to an urban setting where everything had to be bought. But even more distressing, we were preparing to enter the work force in the industrial sector, very systematic and codified in its structure; very different from the open modes of work in an agrarian system.

My mother had found a solution for my drinking needs. My grandmother had an old thermos that I could use for American coffee. American coffee became my standard drink for coffee breaks and lunchtime. It was a big switch from espresso coffee. It provided me with the fluid I needed during the entire day.

Hertlein was a big blessing for me. Not only did it satisfy my urgent need for work, I was able to easily reach it from my house.

From 242nd Street I could walk down to 1st Street and after about a one-mile walk I was on 4th Avenue in Mount Vernon. I didn't have a car, but I didn't need one and I did not even have to take public transportation.

At dinnertime that evening, we were all more relaxed. The kids, too, realized the meaning of that job. While sitting at the table and eating, we talked about my work, the machines, and the pay. We again tried to figure out how much I was going to earn per week. We were in a state of collective euphoria and wanted to be precise about the amount I would make. Nino took a pencil and a piece of paper and started to solicit the numbers: pay per hour, number of regular hours, pay overtime per hour, number of hours overtime. "Seventy-three dollars and twenty cents," exclaimed Nino. "That's what we will have at the end of the week."

That was not going to make us millionaires, but it was going to be the beginning of financial independence. The fact that we did not have a penny was not affecting our morale. Being without a car became frustrating at times, but it never created anger or disappointment. We survived without a car for three years. We walked to shopping, to church, and to work. Mount Vernon was easily accessible on foot. We were used to walking long distances because in Italy we did not have a car either. The difference was that in Italy all our friends and most of our acquaintances did not have a car; in America every family had at least one car and that made us feel different.

I never felt, however, that we were poor. No house, no car, no money in the bank and we never felt that we were destitute. I believe that poverty is not just an economic condition; it is, above all, a state of mind, a psychological condition that dries up all desire and hope to move on. In our case and that of most emigrants, the zero economic level is felt as a base to restart, to reshape or reconstruct one's life in the firm belief that with work and determination a better life is not merely possible but is achievable. It is from that determination and strong belief that one is able to undergo and willing to accept the most difficult, dangerous, and sometimes humiliating challenges. It was just a matter of time, but I knew that we were going to have our own house, our own car, and that we would attain a college education. These things were not vague dreams; they were objectives that we were set to accomplish with determination sustained by a burning desire. The question was how to get there. In retrospect, it is interesting to watch how at that economic stage, in the humblest social conditions, anxious desires for material well-being originate and develop, as well as the perturbations caused in a family, which had until then lived in relative happiness, in a vague yearning for the unknown and the realization that one is not so well off but could be better off. It was a family yearning, not a simple individual desire.

FIVE

On Monday morning I got up when the alarm rang at seven; while my mother prepared breakfast, I got ready. I quickly ate something, grabbed the bag, and left. My mother came down stairs and stood in front of the building. "*Dio ti benedica*" ("God bless you"), she said and followed me with her eyes while I was walking down 242nd Street. I left reassured by my mother's blessings. Although I am relatively short, I could walk fast and was able to cover the mile or mile and a half distance in less than half an hour.

I was very happy that I was starting to work. I had never thought that I would be doing that kind of work. I could not, however, pretend to expect better: I did not speak English and I did not have skills. Most of all, I could not waste time looking for a job that I liked while my grandparents were supporting the eight of us.

Going to work I was tense not knowing how the day was going to evolve. Thinking about my grandfather when he came to America alone at age 16, without having any skills and just with an elementary-school education, I felt that I had some distinct advantages. And I did. I knew that I was much better off than millions of Italian emigrants who had preceded me even in recent years. I was not part of any business deals between Italy and the United States as it had been for thousands of emigrants who, for example, went to Belgium and Holland in the 1940s. I remembered reading in the newspaper that in 1946 the Italian government made a deal with the Belgian government to exchange Italian emigrant workers for a set amount of Belgian coal. As a result of the bilateral agreement, every week 2,000 new Italian workers would be transferred from Milano to Belgium by train. Many of them paid with their lives for the coal that was being sent to Italy to help the industrial reconstruction after WWII. Going to work that morning I was thinking about those casualties from a mining accident in 1956 at Marcinelle that caused the death of 262 miners; 136 were Italian. Those Italians and many others in mine-related accidents in France and Switzerland nine years later paid dearly for the Italian economic miracle. Up to the 1960s, Italian migrant workers, and migrant workers in general, were particularly vulnerable to accidents in the workplace and received very little protection against them. Poor working conditions had led to a high number of fatal accidents that claimed a great number of Italian workers' lives. Fortunately, I did not face those conditions. Going to work I felt lucky to be employed in a machine shop with health insurance and to be paid time and a half for overtime. I had a job with no dangers and was close to home.

When I arrived at the factory, Hewey was there already. He took me down to the basement and showed me where to change into work clothes and where to leave personal belongings. Some men were already getting changed. I watched discreetly and tried to do the same. I hung up my clothes and put on the work clothes and shoes. We took our bags with lunch upstairs. Upstairs, Hewey showed me a box containing a jig for the machine parts that I had to drill for the first job. It also contained the blueprint of the machine parts. The company built machines that made drill bits.

It was an easy job. I had to clamp a metal part in a vise and drill precise holes. It was work that was done with bare hands; no one wore gloves. I discovered quickly that I had to endure some discomfort working at the drill press because the metal chips were very hot and very often they fell on my hand holding the vise. Over the next two years that I worked at that machine, my left hand always had red burns caused by the hot chips. It was a small price to pay to hold that job.

Around 9:40 a truck arrived, gave two calls with the horn, and several people went to the front of the building to buy coffee and bagels or croissants. I pulled out my first cold-cut sandwich and the thermos and had my first coffee break. At lunchtime most of the people took out their own sandwiches with Wonder Bread and sat at their benches. I pulled out my two long sandwiches with Italian bread; I put them on the bench and started to pour coffee.

The two sandwiches caught the eyes of one of the guys who made a remark I could not understand. Before I knew it, three or four guys were looking at my two sandwiches; it seems that they were amazed by how much I was eating. They were probably even more amazed later on to notice that I was losing weight even though I was eating that much.

At the end of the day I changed and went home where my mother and siblings waited anxious to know how the day went. I explained everything, and I did not miss telling them how amused my co-workers were at my sandwiches. And so the kids wanted to know what they were eating to find my food so funny. "No, it was not so much what I was eating that amused them," I said laughing, "it was the amount I was eating."

As the time passed and my communicative skills in English started to develop, work became more enjoyable and life became easier. After a week there, I discovered that one of the guys, on his way home, passed very close to Roosevelt High School in the Bronx and offered to give me a ride to school. I had started to take English and a speech class, and I had to be there at seven o'clock. It was perfect: We finished working at six thirty and at seven I was in class. At ten I would finish, catch a bus and be home by eleven. It was a miracle to have transportation from the factory to school. After a couple of months, when I had some money, my mother told me to offer Joe a couple of dollars for gasoline; but he refused it saying that I was good company and it gave him chance to practice his Italian.

At Hertlein I met some people who were wonderful to me. During lunch I spent a lot of time with Stanley. He had come from Czechoslovakia and had full control of English. He would go over the pronunciation of the English words I was learning and help me with the spelling. I did not have much time for studying, so I would use every spare moment I had at lunch and on weekends. I remember taping a list of English word assigned for homework on my bench or in front of the drill press and memorizing them and then, during the break, Stanley would test me.

I had the impression that Hertlein hired only Germans and Italian Americans. Several employees had recently come from Germany; but among the Italian Americans I was the only one who was born in Italy, the rest were second- and third-generation Italian Americans. They did not speak Italian, but most spoke dialect and tried to communicate with the few words or expressions they had learned from their parents or grandparents. And I had the sense that they were savoring those words, buried down in their memories, as if their word, connected them to a cherished experience.

As every Italian, in those years, I was bilingual; my first language was Beneventano, a dialect very close to Neapolitan, which we spoke at home and in ordinary conversation. Then there was standard Italian, which we learned at school and used in formal situations. In America we had to make some adjustment in our speech and communications. At Hertlein I had to adjust to a mixture of dialects. Joe, Hewey, Nick, and others were second- and third-generation Italian Americans whose grandparents and parents came from different parts of Italy and, therefore, spoke different dialects or a blend of dialects. It was natural that their "Italian" very often could not be connected to a particular area or region. My Italian American coworkers did not know all this and lived with the impression that they knew Italian or an Italian dialect and I never tried to correct their belief for fear of embarrassing them and wounding their pride.

However, one day I was confronted with an embarrassing situation in communicating with Hewey. I had made a terrible mistake and had ruined a job; I was at the point of being fired. Hewey, George, and Mr. Hertlein came to see me. I was terrified. Mr. Hertlein looked at the part in the metal box. Hewey started to yell in his Italian and wanted to know how I could mess up so badly. "*Ai ruinato 'na giobba de tre mila scudi,*" I remember him saying. He spoke a mixture of Italglish, Neapolitan, Sicilian, and other creations. And he was pestering me with questions and cursing the day he had hired me. I was stunned. These guys not only are going to fire me, I thought, but they are also going to make me pay for the damage. "*Strunzu, nun dici nient. Ma capisci u Talian.*" I was not answering not only because I was scared but also I could not understand well what he was saying. I was almost tempted to say, "I've had enough of your arrogance and meanness, keep your lousy job and find someone else who is willing to be subjugated to your damned way of vilification."

I survived that terrifying moment for two reasons. My mother had taught me not to react by impulse, to bite my tongue and express my feelings only when my brain could prevail. But I also restrained from reacting because I needed the job and I could not afford to waste time looking for something else. Thank God that I chose to be silent. Meanwhile, Mr. Hertlein was looking at the jig. He took the jig and inserted into it one of the parts I had ruined. He discovered that the part could be inserted in the jig two ways. Man, he became furious with George and Hewey. They all left and I remained waiting for the next box of parts.

Later, during the coffee break of the afternoon, I was told by Nick that the boss had yelled at both George and Hewey for having made a jig which allowed making holes and boring in two different ways. Normally, parts could be fit into a jig in only one possible way. It was a lesson for me. From that day on, I did not rely exclusively on the jig, but I also checked the blueprint.

Hertlein Special Tool, Co. was privately owned. The founder and owner, Mr. Carl Hertlein, was a mechanical engineer who had been able to create an enterprise that employed about seventy people, mostly machine tool operators and tool and die makers. Building machines required precision, dedication, and reliability. Before reaching the assembly area, parts went through several steps; the last one was the grinding where the internal parts of the machine were honed to precision to fit or connect to other parts. The company had been able to hire mostly terrific, hardworking, and loyal workers and did its best to keep the morale up.

I quickly learned that the boss wanted to have a personal relationship with his employees and make his benevolence felt. The Wednesday evening before Thanksgiving, as we left from work, he stood at the exit, shook hands, wished us and our families Happy Thanksgiving, and gave us a turkey. When my turn came, he said, "Mario, wait, let me find a big one for you. You have a very big family." I was amazed to see my big boss, Mr. Hertlein, search for the biggest possible turkey for my family. I was touched by that kindness and generosity. I thought, "What a man! This is incredible. I am nobody and he cares about my family."

Walking home with the big turkey, I was reflecting on my generous load. "What a country this is, people pay attention to you regardless of where you come from or who you are. He could have given the big turkey to his favorite employee, probably to his foreman. Instead, he considered need as his priority." When I arrived home, I was happy to make an entrance with the big "trophy." "What's that?" my mother asked before I was able to say anything. In putting the turkey on the table, I was tempted to play a prank about it; but my mother had strong intuitions. "Who gave it to you?" And we spent the evening talking about American generosity. That day we received by mail a box of apples with no note inside. We thought that it had been sent by our relatives from Boston because it was shipped from there. When I went to work after the long weekend, I learned that the apples were part of Mr. Hertlein's benevolence.

My grandparents had already bought a turkey, but they decided to cook my turkey because it would have provided abundant meat for the entire extended family which for this occasion also included the Lonardos. This was the first of many holidays that we all spent together at 242nd Street. For us it was a new holiday, which introduced new dishes and new traditions. We were not used to eating turkey with gravy, stuffing, cranberry sauce, sweet potatoes, corn, mashed potatoes, and pumpkin pie. My brothers and I struggled with the food; we wanted to be appreciative of the abundance and thankful for being together, but our palates and stomachs were not cooperating. My siblings got up a few times with the excuse to go to the bathroom or for something else so that the attention would not fall on their still full dishes. We tried to create other distractions by asking explanations on the origins of the holiday and on the tradition of those particular dishes. We all agreed that was a wonderful holiday: no gifts, no pressures of going to church or other social or religious obligations. It was a truly wonderful holiday also because it brought a long and restful weekend. For me it was a welcome break from the factory and school at night.

I had been working about two and half months at the factory and had gotten used to the routine: walk to work in morning, use lunch and coffee breaks for school work; at six-thirty Joe would give me a ride to Roosevelt High School on Fordham Road; at about ten o'clock classes were over, catch the bus and be home by eleven. Usually my mother was waiting for me sitting in the living room, sometimes snoozing; as I entered, she would jump up and we moved to the kitchen. She would take the dish of food being kept warm on the pilot of the stove, place it on the table, and sit with me. I understood that she did not want me to eat by myself and she would engage in conversation. She wanted to know how the day went, what we had done in my classes, and then she would tell me about my brothers and sisters.

After a couple of months, I was asked by the foreman if I wanted to work a couple of extra hours on Saturdays to sweep the factory with another couple of guys. Naturally I accepted; I could add almost four dollars to my weekly pay. I had already received a ten cent raise and was taking home almost eighty dollars. We were paid on Fridays each week. I would routinely sign the check and give it to my mother. We were able to meet immediate needs and save a few dollars.

Christmas arrived. We were happy about the way Americans prepared for the holidays. We did not have a social life, but there was a lot of activity in the family. My time out was with my cousin Gianni who often went to City College on Friday evenings where there were many cultural and social events.

Two days before Christmas, Mr. Hertlein again gave us a turkey just like Thanksgiving, and again it was a big surprise for my family. We worked half a day and then went to a restaurant in Yonkers for the company Christmas party. It was a wonderful party. I was again exposed to new foods and drinks. When it came to our choice for dinner, I was lost, but my Italian American co-workers convinced me to order lobster. Not only was it a completely new dish, but I learned that it was an expensive one. Although it was practically an all-male event, we had a fantastic time. One guy played piano very well and several others sang Christmas carols as well as other songs. When they did a couple of Neapolitan songs, they pulled me in and I led the singing. It took some courage because I, like the rest of the Mignones and, for that matter, the Iannaces, can't carry a tune. Going home I thought about the camaraderie of my coworkers and the generosity of Mr. Hertlein. I thought that labor unions were not always a necessity.

Riveted to the machine and working with all my energy, I was satisfied with what I was doing, but I was determined that it was not going to be my life's work. We didn't have a union and, therefore, did not have a bargaining agent. Pay increases were handled on an individual basis. After five or six months I felt that I was working very hard and deserved a big increase and decided to go to speak directly to Mr. Hertlein. I gave him the talk I had rehearsed a couple of times with my cousin Gianni: "Mr. Hertlein I respectfully would like to ask that you consider giving me an increase. I like working here; I like what I do and work very, very hard. I only go to the bathroom when I need to but I never stay there twenty minutes. I think I deserve more money." He listened with a very serious face and quickly replied, "Mario, I know that you work hard and we appreciate it. You have not been here very long," and he paused. "O.K., I will give you fifteen cents more." I was happy, but the offer did not completely satisfy my expectations. "Thank you, Mr. Hertlein, you are very nice. But I think I deserve more. Mr. Hertlein, I would like twenty-five cents. I need more money for my family." I could see that he was visibly touched and said, "Mario, I know your condition. I will give you twenty-five cents, but don't tell anyone. Did you understand me?" "Yes. Thank you, thank you very much. I promise you that I will continue to work very hard," and went back to work.

Unfortunately, I did not keep my promise because I was very happy and the only way I could have real satisfaction was sharing my secret with someone. I made the terrible mistake of revealing it to a coworker who, I thought, could be trusted. I created problems for myself and for Mr. Hertlein. In no time my increase became the gossip of the shop. Some people secretly went to make their pitch for their own increases; others overrun by their envy and jealousy played some ugly tricks on me. One day, when I returned from the bathroom I found the handle of my machine full of grease. I learned a lesson that shaped my behavior for a good part of my life: If you don't want something to be known, don't reveal it!

Most of the co-workers worked hard, but a guy working at one of the lathes always complained about everything. Often he went to the bathroom taking the newspaper and stayed for a long time. I found his behavior very disturbing but I kept my feelings to myself. Everyone, including the foreman was aware of his demeanor; and it seemed that no one was giving it any attention. However, one morning around nine o'clock the foreman went to him, gave him a check, and asked him to gather his tools and leave the shop. It was clear to me that he had been fired. He was two machines away from mine. He said a couple of vulgarities and started to gather his tools. I was trying to see what was going on and looked sideways. The foreman stood there watching the guy collecting all his belongings; he did not move one inch. After about half an hour, the man, with a toolbox and other belongings, walked toward the exit and George followed him: He was being escorted to the exit.

During lunchtime I learned that he had worked at Hertlein for over fifteen years. I learned that longevity did not mean anything. Without a bargaining agency, the boss had the authority to fire his employees whenever he wanted. I had mixed feelings about the incident. On one hand, I was almost pleased that the guy had been given a lesson. I felt that if he didn't like that job, he should have gone elsewhere to make a living. He had not been forced by anyone to be there. On the other hand, I was shocked by the way he was thrown out the door.

This incident left an impression on me for many years to come. There is no question that Mr. Hertlein treated his employees with dignity and cared about their wellbeing. Overall, he was able to keep the morale high and enjoyed our respect. Most of my colleagues understood that as employees we had responsibilities and duties. However, I also thought that an agency, an organization, or institution had to protect the rights of the workers; workers deserved equitable compensation and a basic welfare protective net. I thought that corporations and small businesses should not be allowed to value alone the labor they consume because they tend to value labor only to create capital. I always thought that the existence of strong labor organizations, such as unions, is necessary to achieve balance in the economy and wellbeing for those who constitute the engine of the economy.

When I was about to leave Hertlein, after a four-year work experience that molded my future behavior in the work place, I had a long discussion with one of my co-workers about unions. We were both immigrants, he was from Germany, and both of us embraced the capitalist system, but he was anti-union by principle.

"You can't be against unions on the assumption that all the American workers are treated like us at Hertlein Special Tool. American workers all over the country are not treated with white gloves. It seems you don't know the labor history and the fight for human and equality rights in this country and what labor unions have contributed to that struggle. Have you forgotten the debt we all owe to the literally dead and wounded union warriors in the long struggle for the ten-hour day, then the eight-hour day, the two-day weekend, and the minimum wage? Unions are all about jobs, wages, security, and working conditions," I said.

"And they also pushed unproductive work rules, featherbedding and job protections that made it all but impossible to fire bad employees. They drove costs up for companies, prompting them to look abroad," my friend replied.

"Do you really believe that workers, even those who are not unionized, would enjoy the protections, benefits, and pay that have today if we did not have unions?" But my friend was too concerned about prosperity as if prosperity was only created with capital and workers' contributions were secondary, ancillary. The premise of collective bargaining is that by representing all employees, a union can negotiate a better collective contract than each worker could get through individual negotiations. He was not taking the next step to see who was going to enjoy the created prosperity and how. I was grateful to Mr. Hertlein for the increases to my hourly wage, but I was not completely happy that I had to go to his office and beg for it. My friend did not like the unions because they negotiated collectively; the same contract covers every worker, regardless of his or her productivity or effort. I closed that discussion with a laconic warning: "The stronger the capitalist system, the stronger the labor unions must be." We remained friends even if we differed profoundly on a vision that profoundly affected our lives.

In retrospect, after so many years in academia and having dealt with labor intellectually and as a small "manager" of an academic department, my position has not changed in time. History and experience have been always my best teachers. Between 1946 and 1973, industrial production doubled in the United States. In those years, workers' incomes also doubled, and the great middle class, the greatest affluence for the greatest number of people, ever, was created: yes, with labor unions. They historically fought the good fight for fair wages, the 40-hour workweek, safe workplaces, pensions, and health insurance.

Anyone who has worked in a large unionized corporation knows that everyone benefits with the efforts of the unions, even non-union employees, and there are often many of them. Corporations do not have to unionize, nor do they want to unionize, all their workers. So they pay them and give them benefits very close to union benefits. The non-union workers in that corporation and other similar corporations get those benefits without a scratch or a scar; but they would not get it if unions did not exist.

The support and protection of unions has become an issue of life and death for the middle class and for the survival of democracy in our country. In 2010 the Supreme Court, in one of its farthest-reaching decisions ever, definitively declared that corporations will be allowed to give money, within campaign contribution legislation, directly to candidates. This means corporations will, in effect, be able to elect their own candidates. This also means that if a mining company wants to blow the top off of a mountain in Pennsylvania, which will destroy the land and water around it, the corporation can buy the politicians and then do it. It could buy the local state senators and representatives, the local member of the House of Representatives, and even the federal Senators.

Coal companies, the major oil companies, utility companies, and the major lobbying firms on K-Street could buy those politicians. But if they found that they could not influence those politicians, they would simply find their own candidates. They have more than enough money and a hundred times more than the unions to fight it. Why would all these firms join in? Because once a politician is on the take, he or she is likely to be on the take from everyone.

Corporations are in an ongoing struggle with American workers. Workers have not had an increase in wages for many years. They have lost millions of jobs to foreign workers. Too bad that I lost contact with my friend at Hertlein; I would love to again take up that discussion of almost fifty years ago that amicably broke up without us finding common ground. I believe that history will prove me correct and, sadly, there is no way that we can sit down with a gin and tonic and talk about our present with the experience of our past, tested by time. However, we will both be correct in remembering Carl Hertlein with admiration and that Hertlein Special Tool was a place of work where people were recognized for their worth and respected for their human dignity.

SIX

In those early months in the Bronx we had to make many adjustments while facing many obstacles and frustrations. We practically lived at my grandparents' house, which was located next to the five-apartment building where we lived and which my grandparents owned. We did not have a television set and because we felt caged in the three-room apartment—we had moved from a farmhouse, which provided a lot of space—when my younger siblings finished their homework they went next door to watch television. Television was a form of entertainment, but it was also an excellent medium to learn English in a household where only Italian was spoken.

Thanks to my Uncle Vincent who was still single and enjoyed home life relaxing by watching television in the evening, my brothers found in him a great guide and companion. He provided for the evening activities, either by entertaining the kids' playing cards or watching television or even going over homework. Uncle Vincent had been in the Korean War and occasionally, under the pressure from the boys, would mention particular moments of that experience. The boys were intrigued by what he had to say, but most of all, by my uncle's conviction that the fighting was necessary. America had gone to a war unprepared and many died or were captured because of poor training and obsolete equipment. Thousands of young people died—their lives cut short. The loss of life seemed tragic and senseless to him, but he also felt that America had to protect democracy and freedom. Uncle Vincent had a strong patriotic streak and was proud of having fought for America, his new homeland. Having been called to duty after only four years in the United States, he served with conviction in the fight against communism, and he fought with distinction.

Sometimes, pressured by my brothers, my uncle would show

some of the pictures he had saved from the war. He had developed many of the photos since he liked photography and learned the skill not only to take pictures from the best possible angles, but also to develop them. "We did save South Korea to be whatever it wanted to be—good or bad," he used to say. One evening he said with firm conviction, "I went and luckily came back. I do feel some modest pride that I was a part of an episode that protected our freedom. If most Americans don't know or don't care, that's O.K. and that's to be expected. The Korean War reaffirmed our strong belief in the ideal that life is not worth living if it is not free." The experience in the war had inculcated in his soul the conviction that it is worth dying for freedom: "Freedom doesn't come for free," he used to repeat occasionally.

Uncle Vincent loved *Bonanza* and all of us, in those initial years in America, developed a love for the show. *Gunsmoke, Mission Impossible, The Fugitive* were standard staples on the screen. I guess the shows with a lot of action and limited dialogue were a perfect language-learning medium for all of us. But in all of them there was also a strong parental role model. Coming from a culture where parental presence in family structure was central, those shows held our attention. *Bonanza* chronicled the weekly adventures of the Cartwright family, headed by the three-times-widowed patriarch Ben Cartwright (played by Lorne Greene). He had three sons, each by a different wife: The eldest was the urbane architect Adam Cartwright (played by Pernell Roberts) who built the ranch house; the second was the warm and lovable giant Eric, "Hoss" (played by Dan Blocker); and the youngest was the hotheaded and impetuous Joseph or "Little Joe" (played by Michael Landon). *Bonanza* was considered an atypical western for its time, as the core of the storyline dealt less about the range than with Ben and his three dissimilar sons, and how they cared for one another, their neighbors, and just causes.

Uncle Vincent had a great ability to keep the kids occupied around him, and the kids enjoyed his fatherly and moral presence. Once, one of the boys found a woman's wallet in the street near home and took it home without opening it. Uncle Vincent sat with him in the dining room, opened the wallet to find some kind of identification. There were several pictures, which indicated that the woman was black and had kids. Among the various papers, Uncle Vincent also learned that she was on welfare. There was no driver license: Not being able to afford a car, probably she did not bother to get it. She lived in Mt. Vernon, apparently, not too far from where we lived, walking from the last subway stop at 241st and White Plains Road to her house where she had dropped the wallet. The wallet also contained $20. But there was no phone number.

The incident provided the opportunity for a good lesson on morality. My uncle and the boys could have turned in the wallet to the police without the $20; the woman would have appreciated the act of generosity because of all the documents it contained and the boys would have had $20 extra to contribute to the family on top of what they were making delivering newspapers. But Uncle Vincent proceeded to tell them what the loss of $20 meant for that woman with children who was on welfare. He went to the phone directory and searched for the phone number of the woman to inform her about the wallet. Finding the number was a big relief and created the biggest excitement for the boys in those early months in America. The next day the lady was going to come to the house to pick up her wallet and they were going to meet her. When she arrived, she hugged the boys and placed a small envelope in the hand of one of them. My uncle told my brother to give the envelope back and, almost begging her he said, "Please don't do that; the boys and I will be offended to be paid for something that is right." She understood and hugged the boys again and left. Uncle Vincent, in turn gave each of the boys a dollar to express his admiration.

Since Aunt Flora had left for the convent, fulfilling an aspiration she had long held, Uncle Vincent was the only family member who could provide guidance for the three boys. In later years, when my father had to give an answer to the fact that no one of his kids went astray, would attribute it to the role played by my uncle: "He was like a hen for those kids. He would keep those boys around him like chicks." There is no question that my father's assessment was right. It could have been very easy for three boys to go off track at that age.

Aunt Flora, off to a convent in Connecticut, was not visible but frequently called on us to carry out some work for the nuns on Sundays, especially painting. For me it was too demanding because Sunday was the only day free to rest and catch up on studying English for my evening classes. But how could we say no to her after she had been instrumental in solving the political puzzle with the American consulate and finding me employment?

Uncle Guy, uncle Vincent's older brother, still unmarried, was completing his PhD dissertation in Italian at New York University. When he had some free time, he would spend it with his fiancée in Queens.

My siblings were not getting much help or support from my sister Matilde and me, the oldest of the group, because we were both working during the day and going to school at night and would not be home until late. They understood, however, why we had emigrated and the path that we had to follow to make it in the new world. As with millions of other emigrants, our decision to leave had been propelled by the anxious desire for material wellbeing. And our experience at arrival reflects the same anxiety and perturbations lived by individuals and families that were moved to emigrate by the same forces of social expulsion.

Until our departure we had lived in relative happiness but there was a vague yearning for the unknown brought on by the realization that we were not so well off, or that we could indeed be better off. There was no rebellion or anger against anything, but a simple desire to change our status, probably to be part of the progress that was stimulating others to move from the countryside to the city or from the South of Italy to the North or abroad. But after leaving home, the arrival at a new destination takes you to ground zero from which you have to restart. To avoid drowning in the initial process of rebuilding the new life you must apply all the energy that you have. And if you drowned, you could pull down everyone around you. Most emigrants, even if they do not rationalize this innate fear, have the strong feeling that the decision to emigrate was charged by a desire not to fail, which is sustained by the initial search to create a secure material base, and then grows and expands into the pursuit of social status. Once the struggle for the bare necessities is satisfied, the search for material wellbeing rises because of the desire to live like others or better.

The search may turn into greed for riches, which may lead one to take the wrong path or into criminal conduct. The yearnings and the ambitions for a better life may become obsessive and consuming. The secret for a happy and successful migrant experience depends on how the dream for success is embraced.

Fortunately my family was never driven by greed for riches. The yearning to have a more secure life was accompanied by a desire to live in a civil manner and to achieve a place of respect in society and public esteem, which social prejudice denies or makes it difficult to achieve. In retrospect it is interesting to see how we, like millions of other immigrants, escaped the obsession of greed and selfishness and placed energy and passion to build our future in the right place. Every impulse of our activities stimulated unconsciously or consciously our desire and search for material wellbeing to realize the lofty ambitions. It happened like a natural flow. When one knows where this immense current of human activity is headed, one certainly does not ask how it gets there.

And so, almost driven instinctively but with the clear set idea of relying on hard work, we moved on. Immediately the task of rebuilding our lives and the world we wanted began. Although we were not mature in years, we were tempered by a life of hard sacrifice lived on a farm and disciplined by the duties of a rural life. We stayed true to our values of personal responsibility and faith. Nothing exceptional. We were united not only in a common purpose, but also by common values — duty, economy, courage, love of family, and, above all, responsibility for oneself. Like millions of other emigrants, we had enrolled in the silent revolution facing great odds without protesting. And we found a gracious nation, which made it possible for many of us to attend college, and we hoped to give the world new science, literature, art, industry, and economic strength. Many immigrants of our generation, exceptionally modest in their lives, have so many stories to tell, stories that in many cases they will never tell, because in a deep sense they didn't think that what they did was that special, because so many others who immigrated here did it too. And so, *we* are telling our story because, in many ways, it reflects the stories of millions of other immigrant lives, faceless heroes whose personal story will never be told.

The best way to represent our collective efforts is through a metaphor from the world of soccer. We were in attack mode. Even though coming from Italy, *catenaccio* would have been easier, since it had been invented in Italy, a defensive attitude would have been a disaster. We had to be on the offense, playing in attack. In life you have to be daring, take chances, be ready for surprises and have the ability to handle them. In our case, like in soccer, to win we had to put trust in the team; the group is more important than an individual player—Helenio Herrera, the great Argentine soccer coach, used to say, "He who plays alone plays for the opponent." For us winning could be achieved like playing in a good soccer team offensively, conquering the field, not being afraid of the opponents, staying in motion, playing to win. The success could be reached relying on good movements, vitality, not being afraid of clashes and new encounters, with the excitement of a hard-fought game.

While I was setting the example for my siblings by working at my fullest capacity and going to school at night, the others, each at their own age level, were doing the same. My sister Matilde was the only one of my siblings who could work full-time. She was aware of our family situation and the inescapable demand it placed on her. She was almost 18 and had to be the second breadwinner. However, she had a lot of pride and gave a lot of importance to appearance. Working in a factory had not been part of her plan; it was too demeaning for her. Since she was a child, she had dreamed of teaching, and now was seeing that prospect compromised. She, too, had to quickly overcome the biggest obstacle—learning the new language.

Toward the end of the first week here, Uncle Guy found a job for her in a dress factory specializing in elegant female clothes. She had never used a sewing machine even though the job was that of a sewing-machine operator. She lasted only one week! It was a week of hell for her. She just could not stand the sight of the place and quit without having another job lined up.

The search for new work started again. After a couple of days she landed a job in a factory where they made robes. Her job was to sew buttons at one machine and make lapels at another machine. It was not a difficult or stressful job; except for Matilde because she felt it was too debasing—it was another job in a factory!

As I had done, she started night school at Roosevelt High School to take English courses so that she could learn English and earn a high school diploma. In those two years that she went to high school at night she must have changed at least five or six jobs. Occasionally she collected unemployment. Of all of us, she was the one that was having the most problems in adjusting. She was literally crying and praying for a more decent life than working in a factory. She wanted to return to Italy and wrote to my father not to sell our property because she wanted to go back to it.

In this regard, we were looking at the present in a completely different way. I had cut the umbilical cord with Italy and was determined to make it here. The work at Hertlein Tools was for me the first phase of a process. Yes, I would have liked a better job, but Hertlein was providing me with enough money to support the family and to start to build the base for our life here. I would have killed myself rather than give up and go back to Italy as a failure. It would have been a humiliating and cowardly act. And I am happy that Matilde, carrying her wounded pride, was able to endure and go forth.

Maria, who had just turned fifteen, was going to school fulltime. But she too was helping to keep the family afloat with a small part-time job. In that first period in America, life was reduced to work and school. And we did not curse anything or anybody for it. The saying "Love the life that you are living and live the life that you love" was remote from our collective consciousness. We were living life aimed at a better future.

For my sisters there was not much to do in terms of social activities. Through my cousins Pupa and Marisa, my sisters had gotten involved in our parish church choir. Once a week, in the evening, they went to Our Lady of Mt. Carmel in Mt. Vernon to practice for the Sunday Italian Mass, which at that time was the most attended. The church choir was the only outlet. Fortunately, there were several young men in the choir, and my sisters and cousins competed for their attention.

Life was not less difficult and challenging for the boys. They had been enrolled in the local public schools and were facing many obstacles, certainly, worsened by their complete lack of knowledge of the language. Nino had been enrolled at PS16 and placed in 6th grade. Domenico had been enrolled in 5th grade, and Biagio, although two years older than Domenico, had been enrolled in 3rd grade. In those years there were no ESL or bilingual education programs. Immigrant students were thrown, as they arrived, into regular classes without knowing English. One can imagine the huge problems that students and teachers had to face. It was a sink-or-swim method.

Bilingual education with all its benefits and drawbacks was alien to education culture in those years. Cultural assimilation also meant forced language learning. However, considering the experience and the latter success of my brothers, I have some reservations about bilingual education. If non-English-speaking students are isolated in foreign-language classrooms, how are they ever going to learn English, the key to upward mobility? I don't dispute the fact that bilingualism doesn't handicap children's cognitive growth; and multiple language skills do not confuse the mind. Quite the contrary: When well developed, they seem to provide cognitive advantages. However, I can argue that even if bilingual education is effective—which I doubt—it is still a bad idea for the country because bilingualism threatens to sap our sense of national identity and divide us along ethnic lines. But most important, children will "pick up" a second language rapidly if "totally immersed" in it. For generations, this philosophy helped to integrate immigrants into mainstream society and to quickly overcome language barriers. However, we cannot deny that because of frustration and lack of help from the education system, disproportionate numbers of immigrant students failed and dropped out of school. Consequently, the sink-or-swim approach was ruled illegal by the U.S. Supreme Court in *Lau v. Nichols* (1974).

Research has shown that the quality—not the quantity—of English exposure is the major factor in English acquisition. Social communication skills—playground English—should not be confused with academic English, the cognitively demanding language that children need to succeed in school. While playground English tends to be acquired rapidly by most children, academic English is typically acquired over a longer period. This explains why it takes second-language learners five to seven years, on average, to catch up with English-proficient peers on tests given in English.

In spite of the rough beginning, the sink-or-swim method worked for my brothers. However, what was most disturbing about the experience of my brothers in school when they started was the lack of sensibility on the part of those in charge in evaluating their capabilities. Domenico, because of the mix-up of classes, two grades above the level he should have been, was labeled as retarded. And even after the mix-up had been clarified, the boys still had not been properly evaluated. They would have been channeled to BOCES (Boards of Cooperative Education Services) if it were not for my Uncle Guy who went to the school to raise hell. Who knows how many immigrant children in those years were unjustly held back or wrongly tracked!

Again, the sink-or-swim education system was good only for those who were motivated and had a strong character, otherwise one could be easily overwhelmed. My brothers had some guidance from cousins of their age. Although Guido was going to Mt. Saint Michael Academy and Agnese went to Our Lady of Mt. Carmel Elementary School, they were good role models and provided precious psychological support and academic help in the first year.

Life outside of school was no more exhilarating than the time spent in the classroom. In our neighborhood there were no Italian immigrants. The Italian Americans in the area were of third and fourth generation and did not speak the language. The three boys were forced to play together and possibly with Cousin Guido when he was available. But even playing was a challenge. We had grown up on a farm where playing and socializing with other kids were not part of our cultural formation. Toys were practically nonexistent, and leisure time had to be stolen from the tasks our father assigned to us: If we were not doing homework, he would quickly find something for us to do. The combination of having lived on a farm, having grown up immediately after the war, and having been raised in a family of eight children had molded our character in a particular way.

Yes, growing up on a farm with no toys and television forced us to learn to use our creativity to find amusement or pleasures. When occasional free time was allowed, we could run around; jump hay bales; climb trees; feed the cow, donkey, and other animals; make forts; and basically play outside in imaginative ways. There is a certain freedom with so much space, peace, and simplicity that we loved.

Living on a farm, your life is molded by the fear of the unknown. As always and everywhere, farmers have to be self-sufficient and resourceful. You are a part of the land you work. You pray and go to church because you are at the mercy of the good Lord. But you also respect God's creation because you are never as close to it as you are on a farm. With your existence at the mercy of Mother Nature, you try to plan for the unexpected and learn to accept disaster with a stoic attitude.

For us, growing up on a farm and participating in farming life allowed us to understand plant, human, and animal relationships, develop a sense of responsibility and an unparalleled common sense, and gain skills and experiences that helped us even if we did not choose to become farmers. There is no question that the life on a farm gave us a predisposition to seize opportunity with preparedness.

My nephew Roberto once said that the Mignones don't know how to relax and don't know how to have a good time. Well, we are not good dancers, we are not good singers or musicians, we are not good swimmers, we are not card players, and we don't know how to do many other things that people usually do to have a good time. But we have many other qualities that made our lives happy and full.

When we came to the United States and moved into an urban environment, we adopted from the new culture those practices and behaviors that did not clash with the culture of the old world and found them enjoyable on our own terms. Naturally, for the younger siblings it was easier to absorb and be absorbed by the new culture, especially when it came to the world of toys, which had not been part of our culture but which now brought a sense of excitement with the things they found to play.

Our approach to the new world can be illustrated with an incident that happened one Saturday afternoon. When I returned from work I found my brother Nino playing on a tricycle he had found in the cellar of the apartment building in which we lived. It must have been left there by one of the tenants, probably to be thrown away because it was too old and too small for their children. It was a tricycle for a child four to seven years old. Nino was thirteen and was struggling to ride it; his knees flapped sideways and his rear engulfed the seat. It seemed to me so idiotic to see him trying to ride such a small tricycle. And then, what the hell was he doing in the street instead of studying or doing some work around the house! I gave him a couple of slaps and sent him inside.

Only years later, thinking about that incident, I realized how ingrained our agrarian culture was in me. It dawned on me that the poor boy was having fun playing with a toy that he never had as a young child. I was still the farmer taking the place of my father: If you finished studying, you must find something productive to do!

The most troubling incident in those first few months happened on a Saturday afternoon. Coming from work, as had become customary, I found my mother next door at my grandparents' helping my grandmother with house chores. She was doing their laundry and crying very discreetly. I was stunned. I had never seen my mother cry. She was a strong woman who had grown up with her father living abroad most of the time and with a domineering mother. Through the years she had endured a tough life that included burying her first three children who died at a very young age. And there she was, now, crying. What could have happened? I didn't think that she was crying because she missed my father. The two of them loved each other, but both could easily endure living apart. And I don't think that she was crying because she missed my brother Enrico: He was studying medicine and was going to be the first doctor in the family! She was not sobbing, not yelling or screaming. No, she was not freaking out. It was a silent, almost a repressed cry. "Holy shit," I thought, "What the hell is this about!"? She wiped her tears, blew her nose, and continued to do the laundry in my grandparents' basement, as if everything was normal. "What do you mean 'it's nothing'? "Ma, what happened? Did you get hurt? " I asked anxiously. "It's nothing, it's nothing," and she was saying it in a dismissive tone as if she had been caught by surprise in a very private moment. I asked two or three more times, but no confession came out.

I went outside and took a walk around the block. I was so disturbed that I could not do anything else. Walking down 242nd Street, I tried to understand what could have hurt my mother that much. Again I thought that she was a very strong woman who was very resolute and determined in her actions. Her life had been tempered by experiences that toughened her character. Mamma was the oldest of six children who grew up practically without a father since he had emigrated to America and every couple of years returned to Italy to leave my grandmother pregnant and to make sure that the family was growing soundly. Being the oldest and without the presence of a father, she had to learn at a very young age how to assume a lot of responsibilities. But her sisters and mother were just as tough. I always wondered how they succeeded in keeping their marriages together for so many years. Their husbands, my father included, lived all their lives with very domineering wives. Of the four sisters, I don't know who was the toughest. And of all the husbands, I believe my father was the least malleable.

The women in my mother's family were not different than many of the women in Southern Italy whose husbands and fathers were living in distant lands. Many of them, besides being daughters and mothers, had to fill the roles left vacant by the emigrated fathers, brothers, and sons. My grandmother, called "the general" by some of us for her overbearing character, had to carry on the role of wife and husband, mother and father. She was more authoritarian than compassionate in her actions.

When my mother got married, not even eighteen years old yet, she was already a well-seasoned woman. She moved into my father's family of all males. Not an easy setting for a comfortable life. Any other woman would have collapsed, but not my mother. After a rough beginning, she earned the respect and admiration of the all-male Mignone clan. And she was able to endure a very harsh farm life to which she was not accustomed. Even worse, she had to suffer the loss of her first three children, Maria, Enrico, and Maria, who died between the ages of 18 and 26 months. Again, not many women can overcome the loss of all three firstborn children, and my mother had without bearing any visible psychological scars or overwhelming others with the pain of her loss. Now, after overcoming so many years of tribulation, she was crying.

At the end of my walk around the block, I came to the conclusion that something hurt her morale. Perhaps my grandmother may have offended her by criticizing the help that she was providing or, probably, she was demanding more. *Nonna*, although very harsh and insensitive, did not mean her words but was very forceful in giving orders. My mother was doing her best to express her gratitude for all the help our grandparents were giving us, but she didn't want to be considered a maid. My mother had a sense of pride and, I thought, did not like to be treated like a servant.

That evening I did not say anything at dinner. I tried to do homework for my evening English classes; but it was difficult to concentrate. The following day, Sunday, at dinnertime I told my mother that with my next paycheck we were going to buy our own washing machine. I would have liked to say, "so that you don't have to go downstairs and be subjected to the tyranny of your mother." Instead I added, "I will ask the guys at work where to get a good deal and what brand to buy." My mother did not object. Her eyes got shiny; at least that was my impression. I thought that for the first time in my life I had succeeded in doing what my mother had been able to do all her life with all her children: look into our eyes to read our consciousness. When we came back from school or work, with her piercing eyes she would take an X-ray of our mood and detect right away if something went wrong during the day. It was this extraordinary perception and sensibility that allowed our home to be a secure castle that provided us strength to overcome any obstacle.

Life went on with each new day bringing the unknown, which required courage and perseverance. Every morning we left home with some trepidation about what we would face during the day.

But we were also charged with the curiosity to learn and the determination not be overcome. And we were ready to learn, to embrace, and move forward.

Thanksgiving came, after two and a half months here. It was truly a new tradition for us and quickly became our favorite holiday in America. Through the years, I have always said: "What an extraordinary invention. What creativity!" We were told that it was a big holiday to thank God for what we had.

We knew that the presence of God was big in this culture. And here, in America, even if you don't have much, one thanks the Lord for whatever you have. On our currency and in our courtrooms, Americans say, "In God we trust." —Sometimes it is one thing to talk the talk; it is a whole other thing to walk the walk by acting worthy of God's trust in us. But Thanksgiving presents us with moral lessons that can help get us there, and Thanksgiving, for our children and us, presents a teachable moment about who we are and what we stand for.

Rooted in the spirit of the Pilgrims who broke bread with indigenous peoples after they landed on America's shores, Thanksgiving is an icon of goodness and decency. In an unpolluted land that presented both opportunity and risk to the Pilgrims, their first instincts were to thank the Almighty for their journey, their destination, and their warm neighbors. For us, who had just arrived from Italy and had found a welcoming and hospitable environment, Thanksgiving had acquired a personal meaning. Certainly, we had nothing in common with the Pilgrims, but we also had much for which to be grateful.

At our first Thanksgiving dinner, my uncles and cousins explained in different ways the American holiday. It was a good lesson in history and morality. We learned that in the spirit of that first encounter, the tradition of Thanksgiving recognized that we are not alone in this world nor on our land, that we are beholden to God, to our families, and to our community. We do not operate as silos, separated from one another by miles of wilderness but, rather, we are united in common traditions, roots, values, and destiny. There was no better lesson of welcome for us immigrants to become part of this land. With a holiday like this, one doesn't need forced assimilation to become part of this country. If you understand the spirit of the holiday, regardless of religious belief, you share in the Spirit of the Nation.

I thought that the Founders recognized this destiny when they wrote the Declaration of Independence, declaring that all "men are created equal, that they are endowed by their Creator with certain unalienable Rights, among which are Life, Liberty and the pursuit of Happiness."

The early thinkers declared America to be the new "Promised Land" because of the opportunities and values it presented. Extending from that, early writers and leaders envisioned that, as the biblical Israelites who traveled from Egypt to the Promised Land, America had a covenant with God to actualize values and principles.

The world at the time of the first Thanksgiving was not a friendly world—it was a world of privilege for the few and tyranny for the many. America changed that picture. In its founding documents, the authors espoused opportunity, equality, fairness, and faith.

But as did the biblical travelers, we have had our struggles with God and eternal values. In the interest of commerce, we instituted slavery. In the interest of expansion, we took over indigenous peoples' lands. In the interest of profit, we oppressed workers. These blemishes on the American character are an undisputed part of history.

Along the way, we have paid dearly to reclaim values and, we suppose, God's trust. Emancipation. Voting rights. Civil rights. Working rights. Safety nets such as Social Security, Medicare, and Medicaid also followed as we and our elected leaders combated bigotry, racism, discrimination, and poverty with our core values.

And every year that we have celebrated Thanksgiving, since that first year, I thought that with so much hanging in the balance, we should remember the values that have rescued us from the brink in the past.

The Thanksgiving dinner of that first year at my grandparents' followed a traditional menu, with some dishes new to us. It was a beautifully set table with a traditional seating arrangement. My grandfather, the oldest, sat at the head of the table and was served first. But before starting to eat, my grandfather gave the blessing. Since the entire family has always been staunch Catholic, everyone participated in the prayer. But my grandfather was a good raconteur and didn't miss an occasion to express his life's view with a religious bent. For us, Thanksgiving was the first occasion to be touched by my grandfather's religious fervor. It was a Thanksgiving prayer in which was mentioned *Equality, Faith, Family, Freedom, Love and Respect, Self-Expression, Doing the Right Thing, Community, Giving Back, the Good Life, Opportunity, and Success.* Every Thanksgiving at dinnertime, I remember that first Thanksgiving and those words of love, brotherhood, and gratitude. These are not religious values, nor are they conservative or liberal, Republican or Democratic, I thought. What a wonderful invention in this culture of immigrants ... and the food was great too!

When I have a chance to give my blessing at Thanksgiving dinner, hopefully with the presence of my grandchildren, I would like to say that they are righteous values that can earn us God's trust and rebuild our trust in each other. If we say, "In God We Trust," then let's mean it by acting in ways that don't violate God's trust or that of the American people. Leaders and people of power should be role models and have a responsibility to lead in a civil, principled, and God-like way. Let's truly be thankful for the country that God has helped us to mold, a country rooted in values and virtues that have inspired the world. Let's not trash it or each other. Let's *live* our values. Our faith and values have been and can again become our grounding elements. If we really trust God, then we must create a country where, because of its people, culture, and deeds, God also trusts us.

But that first Thanksgiving is also memorable for the novelty of the dinner of the traditional foods that were prepared for the celebrations. It was a dinner with a combination of old Italian dishes—luscious lasagna, eggplant parmesan with loads of cheese, stuffed mushrooms—and typical American dishes for the occasion—turkey, stuffing, gravy, sweet potatoes, cornbread, mashed potatoes, cranberry sauce, and pumpkin pie with fruits, nuts, pastries, and homemade cookies. For me, the cranberry sauce and pumpkin pie were dishes that required years of trial before I started to enjoy them. In those first years I was amazed by what Americans were eating. Peanut butter and jelly sandwiches on mushy white bread! Even some Thanksgiving dishes, in spite of my great attachment to the holiday, have remained outside of my preferred food choices.

SEVEN

There was not much free time those first years in America. Hertlein Special Tools took practically all my time and energy, and evenings were spent taking English courses. Weekends were short and were used to catch up with schoolwork and family business. Friday night was occasionally a big night; it was the night out with my cousin Gianni at the Italian Club at City College, an experience that affected my life profoundly.

My first night at City College was my first night out since we had arrived from Italy. It was September; we had been in America for about three weeks when Gianni informed me that we were going out that Friday evening. I was concerned about how much money I was going to need. I had received two weeks of pay, but I had given the checks to my mother for the family. Gianni was very sensitive and supportive and always made me feel at ease about money. He announced in his jovial way, "Mario, we will go to the pizza party organized by the Italian Club at City College. You will meet a lot of guys who have recently arrived from Italy and are studying there."

I was tremendously excited to make some acquaintances outside the circle of people from the factory where I worked. Although most of them were affable and both helpful and supportive, I was not making any effort to establish friendships or to create relationships among the shop workers for socializing. At the end of the day and at the end of the workweek each went his own way and saw no more of the others until we met again at the factory the next morning.

On that Friday evening, as I finished work, I walked home as usual, showered and shampooed very well to take the smell of factory oil and burning metal off of me, and dressed in the only suit I had. I must say that I looked presentable. My mother reassured me that I looked handsome and I was going to be a hit with the girls. For the first time I was not worried about communicating. Gianni came with his old blue Ford and off we went. "Mario," he said, "I am the president of the club and I am in charge of buying the pizza. I have already ordered fifteen pizzas. We will pick them up on our way to school."

We stopped at a pizzeria, located about a fifteen-minute ride from our house. The pile of pizzas was on the counter waiting for us. Gianni called for Luigi and in Italian asked for the receipt and paid in cash. We put the hot boxes in the trunk and took off. That was my initiation into the world of academia in America. It was the beginning of a journey that lasted all my life.

Driving to City College, Gianni tried to educate me about college life, the presence of many clubs on campuses, social events, and how to succeed with girls. "American girls," he said, "are easily approachable, jovial, cheerful, and if you are patient and know how to be smooth, you can even end up in bed with them. Italian girls are not so easy for sex." It sounded wonderful to me because in Italy girls were not very easy to approach.

At a certain point, Gianni said, "We are in Harlem. This is a black area. City College is here in Harlem." It was dark, but anyone could notice that the area was populated exclusively by blacks: in the streets, in the stores, coming in and out of apartment buildings. It was shocking for me to see such a segregated population in the heart of New York City. I knew that the American population included a large percentage of blacks; I also knew that in the South there still was segregation, but I did not know that in the middle of our city there was such a huge island of blacks.

"Here on the left is Shepard Hall," Gianni said assuming almost the tone of a tour guide, "the largest building and the centerpiece of the campus; it was modeled after a Gothic cathedral plan, and it has a large chapel assembly hall called 'The Great Hall,' which has a mural painted by Edwin Blashfield called 'The Graduate.'" It was an impressive sight. Up to this point the American architecture to which I had been exposed had collided with an Italian sense of design and architectural beauty that balanced with functionality. Shepard Hall and then Harris Hall shook up my early assumptions about American disinterest in aesthetics and sole interest in practicality and functionality.

When we arrived at a gate, Gianni drove in. Stopped by the guards, he said matter of factly, "Italian Club," and was given the OK to move ahead. Surprised by the simplicity with which we passed the "check-point," I asked, "Who is allowed to park inside the campus? Presidents of clubs?" He answered with a smile, "I will show you how it works once we get inside."

After we parked the car, we picked up the boxes and entered the building. "This is Finley Student Center," said Gianni, "the building where students have social events and where we have our club offices." We climbed the stairs to the second floor to a room where there were some young ladies and a couple of guys arranging tables and chairs for the party. Gianni said, "*Ciao*" to the group and then turned to me and said, "Take a pizza and follow me." We went to the gate and Gianni asked the guard, "Is the sergeant around?" "Yes," the guard answered, "he just stepped out. I will call him." As the guard arrived, Gianni asked me to hand him the pizza: "Sergeant, the first pizza is for you. Enjoy it with your friends while it's still hot. If you have a chance, pass by for some Italian coke." I did not get the joke about the "Italian coke," but the sergeant chuckled. As we left Gianni said in Italian, "I wanted you to hand him the pizza so that he gets to know you and when you have the car and come by yourself you don't have to struggle to find parking in the street."

The exchange with the guards left me amused but it also engendered some reflections. I was surprised to see how my cousin and his friends of the club had made connections. The guards were black, but apparently human bonds were not impeded by racial differences or cultural diversity. The pizza in 1960 had not yet replaced hot dogs as the most popular fast food in America, but there were strong indications that pizzerias were going to be spread throughout America and would become a popular food.

Once we got upstairs, I realized that it was going to be a full-blown Italian *festa*. The number of students had doubled and they were all at work decorating the room. Italian colors were all over in every shape and form: red, green, and white; streamers festooned from the ceiling; tablecloths in national colors. A record player was playing Italian and Italian American music; "*Volare*" had arrived in United States and *"Torna a Surriento"* was still popular. Gianni introduced me to various guys and girls, most of them immigrants from Italy or children of Italian immigrants. I was in paradise: I could speak in Italian and talk about things that were meaningful to me. I met a number of people with whom I established strong friendships and, with some, lifetime friendships. I met Leo Cimini, Francesco Raimondi, the Sclafani brothers, Ido De Carolis, Peter Palladroni, Vincenzo Sottile, Linda, Maria, Rosa, Anna, Italia, AnnaMaria, and many more. There was also Rocco whom I had already met at Gianni's house. It was an overwhelming evening and I felt like I was home in a land that still was so different from Italy.

Most of the students were studying to earn degrees to teach Italian and/or Spanish. They were enrolled in the Evening Division because they were working full-time during the day — at that time there was a distinct division between evening and day students. The evening students were self-supporting and some, like me, had to also help support their families. These were kids making it on their own; with that fire in their bellies they were trying to mold a better future for themselves and their families.

The first night at City College I met also Giuseppe and Italo Battista, two young men with whom I established a friendship that lasted a lifetime. They had come ten years earlier by boat, the *Saturnia*; when they arrived, Giuseppe was fourteen, and his brother Italo sixteen. A week after their arrival, they enrolled in an evening adult education course to learn English. Before leaving for America they had studied English in Italy for few months, but it was not enough to speak and understand the language here. The course they took proved to be very beneficial; in fact, with the acquaintances of new friends who only spoke English, they were able to practice and learn the English language fast. Another factor that helped them learn the language was that they lived near a movie house, and they would go see American films at least three times a week during the first year of their arrival.

In the middle of the 1950s, the Battista brothers were accepted at CCNY as non-matriculated evening students. At that time the college had high and rigid acceptance standards and it was difficult to be accepted as a full-time matriculated student; besides, they could not afford to pursue full-time studies. This was the road on which most of the immigrants embarked. In the case of the Battistas there was also another major problem: Their father had died after few months in America, and consequently they had to work in order to help their mother with the financial needs, pay for school tuition, and provide for their personal expenses.

Giuseppe had found a full-time job as a jeweler in the diamond district at 47th St. in Manhattan, and his brother Italo had found work in an import/export firm also in Manhattan. They worked from 9-5, took the subway straight to 125th and Convent Ave. At 6:00 they were in class at City College; many times they were so tired after a full day's work, that they could not keep their eyes open in the classroom. Like most of the other Italian friends, Giuseppe and Italo ended their classes at 10:00 p.m., after which they got home at 11:00 where their mother was waiting for them with dinner.

Joe was always expansive; in that first encounter he told me so much about his life and that of his friend at the club. I was anxious to see how they were making it and, thus, how to prepare for my college education. Joe said that the City College experience was unique and significant for them; most importantly, it taught them the value, the struggle, and the importance of a college education; they were aware that to get ahead in life a college degree was necessary and they made every effort to achieve their goals. It also taught them the importance of mingling with people of different races and cultures; the majority of the student body at City College, at that time, was of Jewish descent. Students of Italian background, a minority on the campus, often congregated among themselves.

Friendships among Italian students grew stronger and stronger to the point that soon they united with the intention to be part of the school life with the same rights that others enjoyed. As their friendship grew, they formed, so to say, a visible bloc and a belligerent front with the intention of claiming their rights and securing recognition. This was difficult to achieve as individuals, but together *"l'unione fa la forza,"* they decided to do something about it.

They came to the conclusion that the best way to be noticed was to be recognized by the evening school administrators, teachers, and others. Suddenly their hopes began to materialize. One night, at a school event in the Finley Student Center, they met an extraordinary administrator named Dr. Martha Farmer who happened to be the Dean of evening students. At first they began to butter her up with praise for the great work she was doing at the College, and then they explained their concerns for being a neglected group on campus. She took their arguments seriously and promised to help them.

Joe was taking pleasure in telling me the story of the way they established their identity on campus. The encounter with Dr. Farmer was a real blessing; the following week she called and informed them about how to form, first of all, an evening Italian club on campus. She told them to draft a club constitution so that she could have it approved by the student government. With her help it was finally approved, and they named the club: "Il Circolo Italiano of CCNY." They were then told to submit a budget requesting funds to run the club's activities and it, too, was approved.

This was the beginning of a new "adventure" for that first nucleus of students from Italy at CCNY. The Circolo was formed during the middle 1950s. Italo Battista was elected president; Sclafani vice-president; De Carolis secretary; Giuseppe Battista treasurer; Raimondo, Italia, and Rosa, in charge of publicity; and Professor Vito Caporale, an evening adjunct history teacher who sympathized with them a great deal, was faculty advisor.

The club began to organize cultural and social activities such as lectures on Italian culture and civilization, dances, and parties; but the two activities that promoted its visibility on campus were: the yearly "spaghetti party," and the "pizza party," activities organized with the help of female Italian students.

These activities proved to be extremely important and beneficial because they gave the students a great deal of recognition; the students invited to these parties, in addition to their main supporter Dr. Farmer, also the teachers of Italian, namely Professors Errante, Luciani, and Milella; they also invited other school administrators such as Assistant Dean Getzoff, Dean Hall, Dean Pease, the president of the evening student council Phil Garcia, and the director of the school's security Mr. Stefanini.

Gradually, their interest moved from the Italian Club to the Student Government. Giuseppe Battista was elected treasurer of the evening student council, and also president pro-tempore. In this position he was able to advance the status and presence of the Italian students on campus and, at the same time lead the promotion of Italian studies; some Italian courses began to be offered also in the evening session.

Parking at Finley Student Center, where most of the activities took place, was very limited; however, Mr. Stefanini, who became a very good friend, warned the guards to give them access to parking as they needed it, and needless to say, the guards were well compensated with frequent boxes of pizza, dishes of spaghetti, and Italian pastries.

Mr. Stefanini did a lot for them; with his authority he even had Giuseppe, his brother Italo, and Tony Sclafani join the Burns Guard Detective Agency, an agency that provided security in private places such as sports complexes, museums, art galleries, fashion shows, expositions, etc. The three of them were given uniforms, and on holidays, during school vacations, and on weekends they would provide security to those places. One can only imagine the three of them in uniform trying to enforce order and discipline in public places!

By now the Italian Club was well established as was the reputation of the Italian group on campus. It participated in many intra-scholastic and cultural activities such as the international night events, conventions, forums, beauty pageants, conferences, and dances. A small group of emigrant students had established a noticeable Italian presence on campus.

Attending the events of the Italian Club at City College on Friday I quickly discovered that the students of the Italian Club were not unique for the social milieu to which they belonged and for the strong instinctive drive to emerge and make a distinctive impact in their communities and society in general. I learned quickly that CCNY was attracting an exceptional body of students who were achieving outstanding accomplishments. City College was known as the Harvard of Harlem.

CCNY was the first tuition-free college in the United States and it always served a large number of children of immigrants (understandably, there were required courses in public speaking: my friend and I had to take four courses in speech). Admission was generally restricted to the top 10 percent of high school graduates (a far cry from the "open door" of later years), and the curriculum was extensive and fairly demanding. I don't know how the faculty felt teaching the sons and daughters of New York's non-privileged who sought a college education, but they gave the institution and the students their strongest commitment. When I later enrolled there, I never doubted their interest in our intellectual wellbeing. No question, it was an extraordinary center of learning for both students and faculty.

In the early 60s the student body was predominantly Jewish, many of whom were from Europe as consequence of war or were second-generation Americans, several of whom were children of Socialist and labor unionists. Some of those young men differed greatly in academic attainment, intellectual capacity, temperament, and aspiration; but the great majority of them shared with the groups an unusual combination of propensities: toughmindedness, an idealism thinly disguised by a proclivity for criticism, a high regard for scholarly and intellectual accomplishment rooted in religious and ethnic tradition, and a strong drive to achieve.

Although the Italian students were severely handicapped by their economic conditions and limited opportunities, and in a good many cases forced to postpone, prolong, or forgo the advanced study to which they aspired, an impressive number above the norm made their mark in a variety of fields. Several professions other than language and literatures were enriched by the achievements of men and women who received undergraduate degrees at City.

My landing at City College was the biggest blessing in my life. Not long after I arrived, while still working in a factory, I attended activities of the Italian Club on Friday evenings where I was exposed to the life of a campus and thrown into a student body that was brewing in and at the same time heating up the air for social change. I am indebted to Gianni, Rocco, the Battistas, the Sclafanis and so many of those young men who took me into an environment that shaped my consciousness, socially and culturally, in my first period in America. Thanks to them, during the day my body was at Hertlein Special Tool because I needed the money, but my mind and my desires for the future were at City College. Even though I was not ready to enroll there, the activities of the Clubs became my main cultural and social interest.

It was the contagious club life that first opened my mind. The large number of clubs offered students opportunities to share common interests and appreciate cultural diversity, to learn how to plan programs and request and manage budgets. Despite the challenges of community, employment, and family responsibilities, students learned a sense of altruism and developed a strong sense of engagement in the life around them. As young immigrants, interest in new ideas was not simply part of the college experience; it was practically the whole of it. If students left City College with a better education than did many students at other supposedly better colleges, it was because the involvement in progressive ideas prompted us to read and think and argue with furious energy. I detected quickly that they liked to argue, and it was practically almost impossible that they would find common ground for agreement. Anyone could join in an argument, and the different views were never pushed for simple personal snobbism. How great it was seeing them fight and getting in the fight!

In retrospect, I believe that those students were truly different from the students at other universities. They had to face the many pressures of metropolitan life. Most of them had been reared in small crowded homes where privacy had been at a premium. Many had to take long rides on subways to and from school. A few had their perspectives on social problems broadened from their experience from abroad. A large majority of them were also first- and second-generation Americans and, therefore, were torn between European and American standards, between the codes and customs of their parents and those of their groups. They came largely from lower-income groups, so that they grew up in homes where there was a continuous and severe financial struggle. Since more than 97 percent of students lived at home, parents usually continued to exercise close supervision over their time, friends, and money.

In general, the experience at CCNY was indeed rewarding for all of us. It made us grow both intellectually and socially. Campus classrooms were overflowing with young men in their mid-twenties, many of whom had never expected to get a college education, and were burning with thirst for knowledge and a desire to change their social status but also societal structures and obstacles that interfered in social mobility. Most of them came to understand the need for federal civil rights legislation and participated in the social and political upheaval of the sixties.

They left the campus with degrees and a determination to make a difference in life. They moved onto the landscapes of education, industry, science, art, public policy, all the fields of American life, bringing to them the same passions of discipline that served them well in overcoming the big obstacles of immigration. They lived in an environment where family values were strong and the future of the individual members of the families was planned with support from parents who sacrificed to make those plans succeed. The success of the children was paramount to success of the family and of the parents in particular.

In retrospect, compared to the students of a later generation, how lucky were they (and I)! They left with degrees that were worth much more than the same degrees that were earned in later years and they did not have debt. When I think about the debt accumulated by the students of my children's generation I don't know whether to put the blame on the students or on the parents, or on the colleges or even on the loan agencies. They all contributed to the culture of borrow and spend. When we went to college we did not have money and our parents had less; however, there was a predisposition to sacrifice in order to earn a degree. It was a family effort to provide a better future for the younger generation through education. It was a matter of priorities, and our folks put education first. Eating out, taking a vacation, buying a new car were not part of the normal thinking in that culture.

Generally speaking, the high cost of education has not been created by a lack of responsibility on the part of parents or poor planning on the part of parents and children; it has to do with the way states fund higher education and the cultural changes of university administrations. State institutions in many parts of the United States have seen their funding cut by cash-strapped lawmakers, resulting in campus budget tightening and tuition hikes.

At the same time, university administrations are bloated with highly paid administrators, deans with several associate deans, in turn with many assistant deans and assistants to the deans. Even worse, university administrators, in their vision for the university, have placed the main role of educating students at a distance. And let's not talk about the millions that are spent on luxurious student unions and athletic facilities. And while research is vital, some effort must be made to distinguish between advancing the frontiers of knowledge, on the one hand, and fruitless pettifoggery on the other. Campuses must renew their focus on teaching as their core mission and exploit the power of the Internet as a cost-effective way to extend their reach. Unfortunately, rising costs haven't necessarily led to rising quality. Students study less than they did in the 1960s, and half fail to get a degree within six years. The use of part-time faculty has boomed. Grade inflation is rampant.

How much we miss the 60s also for these changes in family and state priorities and in the total vision of what creates a better society through a democratic education system. We at City College were particularly lucky for the students of that era and for the vision of the college administration and the support it received from city and state.

In the fall of 1961 the original "clan" of the Italian Club began to break up. Tony, Ido, and Frank were drafted into military service. Giuseppe applied for a scholarship at several schools; it was the only way to seriously continue his education. One day, in the summer of 1961 he received a letter from the chairman of the Foreign Languages Department of Rutgers University, Professor Remigio Pane, who wanted to interview him. He went to Rutgers, all excited, and his brother went along. They had a long warm chat with Professor Pane who asked about their studies, their life experience at work, and their plan for the future. He seemed to like Joe's résumé and, at the same time, asked his brother if he would be interested in applying as well; Italo told him that he would consider it, and after a couple of days he sent in his application.

Much to their joy and surprise, a few days after the interview, they both received a letter from Professor Pane notifying them that he was offering each of them a teaching assistantship for two years with free tuition and a salary. They were ecstatic. They could not believe that they were going to be paid to study!

Thanks to their new "benefactor," Professor Pane, in two years Giuseppe earned his master's degree, while his brother Italo continued for a PhD.

Their experience at City College, followed by that at Rutgers, "paved the road" and "opened a door" for scores of Italian students to achieve higher-education degrees. Throughout the sixties and a good part of the seventies the road to success was City College-Rutgers. We knew that Columbia and NYU existed, but we did not even try to go there; somehow we felt that Rutgers and City College, as public institutions, would be more welcoming to immigrants. Right after Joe and Italo, the Sclafani brothers went, followed by my cousin Gianni, Bob Bongiorno, Nick Patruno, Antonio Negovetti, Romeo De Rose, Vincenzo Bollettino, and so many others. I followed their path in the spring of 1967, when I graduated from City College.

It seems that America was made for us and we were made for America.

EIGHT

Things were moving along rather well. It seemed we were following a natural course; the current of survival energized by a natural yearning to be better off was sweeping us along in an unexpected flow that was making us overcome the unglamorous trials and tribulations with an instinctive drive not to leave space for questioning life's social disparities. Together, individually and collectively, we were trying to find a way to move forward as a family. Each of the siblings, too young to work full-time, found a small job to add support for the survival of the family. Maria worked in Matilde's factory a few hours a week, Nino found a job stocking food on shelves in a local supermarket, and Biagio became a paper boy. Nino particularly helped with the welfare of our family because, besides bringing home some money, he brought food. Every evening the owner of the family supermarket, aware of the needs of our family, would give my brother those perishable foods that could not be kept for next day: vegetables, fruits, bread, dented food cans, and all sorts of other goodies. At thirteen Nino was providing astonishing support to the family, thanks to the generosity of his boss. We were not swimming in gold but we were managing well and were able to buy those necessities for the apartment that made living more comfortable.

My mother was the banker and manager. Whenever we were paid, we would systematically bring the check or cash to her. "A dollar is made of one hundred pennies," she would remind us, therefore, every penny was valuable. Within the first month she opened a bank account at Eastchester Savings Bank; not only was the account the family piggy bank, it was also the mechanism to cash my and Matilde's paychecks. It had become a routine: Every Friday evening, when I arrived home, I signed the check and passed it to my mother. In turn she would give me five or six dollars, money I needed for the week. Mostly what I needed was to buy subway tokens to get home from Roosevelt High School on Fordham Road. I did not smoke, I did not drink, and I did not have any free time that required spending money. Going out was limited to going with my cousin Gianni to events of the Italian Club at City College. In case of emergency, I had a twenty-dollar bill hidden in my wallet.

In those years we did not have to worry about parental involvement in our key decisions. Our home was like a beehive where everyone worked with the same intensity for the same purpose. Somehow, we did not need to be stimulated to find a job, to work, or to study. All these things were part of a survival instinct. There was no need and no danger for my mother to be "overparenting" and affect our maturity and courage. We learned independence, developed confidence, and acquired skills to bounce back after a defeat. Looking back at those difficult years I feel lucky that my parents did not and could not jump to assist us to remove any barrier or discomfort for us and, thus, rob us of the opportunity to learn how to solve our problems. No one of us was bestowed with poor resilience, a sense of entitlement, high anxiety levels, poor life skills, and an inadequate sense of responsibility.

Regardless of how old we were, we were aware that our family could survive and, possibly, prosper only if we gave our best collective support. We knew that there were some social safety nets that could have assisted distressed families; but it would have hurt our pride just to think about it. My family had always cherished family pride; my father always reminded us where the Mignones came from: "They never worked for anybody and never had debts." The family farm the Mignones owned and worked at Petrara provided the basic family needs and a respectable social standing. The farmhouse had a tower with holes all around for a couple hundreds of pigeons to hide or lay eggs. Those pigeons usually flew as an army on the surrounding territory reaching as far as four or five miles from the farmhouse. Everyone knew that those were the Mignone pigeons and for the Mignones it felt like having their presence all over the hills surrounding their properties. Coming to America we found ourselves at ground zero owning nothing. However, not having a car, not having a washing machine, clothes drier, dishwasher, a bank account with some money, did not make us feel poor. Poverty is also a state of mind. It is the state of mind that holds people depressed, angry, bloodless. We had pride, a sense of self-esteem, decorum, and a determination to make it. One thing was for sure, we had not emigrated to downgrade our social standing. Personal responsibility was our driving force.

We had learned that moral and social standing don't have absolute values; they are mostly molded by culture. For sure personal responsibility is valued differently in the various cultures. I experienced this principle in my dealings with the IRS.

Coming from Southern Italy, it was natural, almost instinctive, that I had to assume the responsibility of providing for the needs of my family. It was not a matter of being a good or bad son or brother. It was the normal way to respond to our situation. When I filed my income taxes, I declared three dependents. My father was still in Italy and my mother had not produced any income since she did not work out of the house; I was the main breadwinner and I felt that the law provided me with the legal rights to have some tax exceptions. Well, I was audited and it was not a pleasant experience every year that I declared the dependents. Frankly, I was not shocked the first year: How can an unmarried twenty-year old claim three dependents? I figured that the IRS needed an explanation.

Although we had been in the United States for about ten months, my English speaking skills were still weak and so I did not feel comfortable going by myself to the hearing. As usual, I asked my cousin Gianni to come along. Not only did he have to help me to explain my situation to the auditor, but he also had to drive me there. Going to the hearing, we engaged in a discussion on the fairness of the taxation system. After so many years, I still remember that exchange. The issue was that though I did not mind paying my share of taxes, I wanted to pay what was fair. What "a fair share" might be is perceived differently by almost everyone.

Because our personal income and that of our families were very low, we were practically supporting each other's point. "I believe that the more income you receive, the more you should pay in 'common charges' to the national enterprises," I said. Gianni reinforced my position with his practical referent: "I don't believe the retired bank teller earning $4,500 a year or my father earning $3,700 should pay at the same rate as Mr. Rockefeller or someone earning $100,000 or $500,000. Put the other way round, I think Rockefeller should pay taxes at a higher rate than his assistants, driver, or maids." "Absolutely," I said, "the burden of taxes on someone earning $100,000 or more per year is far less onerous than the burden on a tight middle-class family budget. Burden counts. But also, someone earning more has benefitted more from the common investments we taxpayers make—roads, transportation, airports, the "common defense," etc.—and so should pay more in return. Look at me, I don't own a car, don't fly, don't take trips, what kind of benefits do I get from the national investments in our infrastructures?" We agreed and got angrier at how unfair the system was. The rich people were getting a higher level of pleasure from what the state was giving for the "common good" while contributing less. "Where is the concept that 'we should contribute according to our ability and benefit according to our needs?'" I said, exasperated. And Gianni to me, "This is not a capitalist concept. Don't forget, we are in America."

Gianni had taught me a trick in communicative skills: how to get by with rudimentary English. He said, "Learn how to use the verb 'to get' and you get everywhere." And I must say that it got me far: "Excuse me, where do I get the bus?," "How do I get more money at work?," "How do I get a new job?" In the first few months it did help me to get by.

After we parked the car, as we were going inside the building, Gianni advised me to focus on explaining how I, the oldest of the siblings, was supporting the family on my low income. At the scheduled time of my appointment, we entered the room and Gianni spoke first to tell the auditor that he was accompanying me because I did not speak English well. I was very nervous and everything was perceived with a sense of threat. I would have liked to melt away rather than face that big representative of a big government. The auditor, seated at the desk, very relaxed, invited us to sit down and asked if we had any records to prove the claims on my returns.

The auditing became an inquest, an investigation into my private life and that of my family. "You claim three dependents... at your age... and without being married," lamented the auditing officer. "How can you explain this; making false statements to IRS may put you in jail," he added. I explained to him the structure of my family indicating the age of each of us. "The youngest is five years old and my mother needs to stay home to take care of the family and house," I tried to stress. "But what kind of support do you provide to the family?" he asked with a firm voice. "Well, every Friday evening, when I get back from work, I sign my paycheck and I give it to my mother," I said as a matter of fact. "Just like that, you sign the check and you give it to your mother?" he asked incredulously. "Yes, just like that, I sign the check and I give it to her every Friday evening," I repeated. "It's impossible that a twenty-year-old gives the entire paycheck to his mother. Don't you go out, don't you buy cigarettes, don't you need pocket money..." and went on trying to understand how much money my mother was giving me and, therefore to find out how much in reality I was contributing to the family. It was an inquest that was both humiliating and irritating. At the end he approved the three dependents with the warning that if I was planning to declare them again the following year, I had to provide tangible evidence. I went home very upset and dejected. I had lost a day of work, worth over twenty dollars, and was given a warning not to abuse the system!

During that year my father joined us from Italy, but his income at the end of the year was less than half of mine and so I continued to give the check to my mother every Friday evening. When the time came to prepare income taxes, I was advised by our accountant to declare two dependents. Again I was audited. Again Gianni accompanied me. My English had improved and I was able to better articulate my explanations. At a certain point, tired of the harassment, I asked him how much more taxes would I have paid if I did not declare any dependent. "We are spending all this time as if I were not paying thousands of due taxes. I am getting tired of this kind of harassment. You know what? I will not give my paycheck to my mother, but the consequence is that my family will start to collect welfare." It was a threat that could never be put into action because of my family sense of decorum, but I could not contain my anger anymore.

The third year, I again declared two dependents and I again was called in for an audit, but this time I was interviewed by a different auditor. We dealt with the same issues and questions. "It's clear that we have a clash of cultures. The average American young man does not live in a big family of young siblings and give the entire paycheck to his mother at the end of the week and so you find my family's way of living strange and suspicious. But even if you find it hard to understand our clannish mode of life, how much money am I not giving to our government? Why don't you call Mr. Rockefeller and try to find out if he is paying his fair amount of taxes. You are looking for the pennies and miss the millions." I got off my chest a burden that I had been carrying for a year. I probably should have been calmer because he was a simple bureaucrat following a tangle of meaningless rules; an employee who was doing his duty on behalf of a system that was screwed up. But was I, a factory worker, able to reach the Director of the IRS and tell him how unjust the whole system was?

Gianni had already taken a course in economics and apparently the professor must have discussed in class the issue of tax inequality. As we were driving home from the third audit for the third year in a row — and I had lost another day of work and Gianni had missed two classes at City College — Gianni brought up the issue of the unfairness of the way investment income was taxed. "You know, Mr. Rockefeller and Company don't make most of their money from a salary earned through work, they get it as investment income. Shouldn't investment income, which is extra income, be taxed at a higher level than the income from work? The overwhelming majority of investment income is received by the richest among us, so there is no strong case for a low rate based on need. And there is no evidence that taxing investment income at the rate of ordinary income produces less investment or fewer jobs. It has been statistically proven that when the investment income tax rate has been low, fewer jobs have been created than when the rate was higher. This suggests that the decision to reinvest in growth as opposed to safety is not primarily a function of the tax rate." It was clear that the economics course had left an imprint on Gianni's thinking.

Going home, I could not understand how this great nation had such an unfair tax system. I could not understand why the IRS was harassing me for having such a low income and so many dependents. If we are at all concerned about hardworking lower- and middle-income people and retirees then we need to pay attention to the rates at which we tax income that they are able to save.

We were happy with our status: We found opportunities to advance. People are not equal: Some seize opportunities, others squander them. Sometimes people complain that the poor shouldn't merely have a chance, but that the government should provide them with a somewhat comfortable life even if they blow that chance.

Going home I became suspicious that these guys were calling me because I came from Italy and that they may have had the terrible prejudice that we Italians don't like to pay taxes and, therefore, should be kept under close scrutiny. In my mind, I was regurgitating over and over this possible prejudice. I could not deny the fact that the bias would have been based on some real facts: Italians, Greeks, and other Southern Europeans are known to evade taxes for a number of various reasons, some of which are historical. But Italians and the others are not different from Americans, I thought, who live surrounded by and contribute to the underground economy. Americans are engaged in large-scale tax avoidance. They do it, I thought, through the political system, and so the only laws they violate are those of fiscal prudence.

When we arrived home, Gianni dropped me off and went to his last class of the day at City College: I had lost a day of work and he had lost a day of classes! There was good reason to be very upset.

As I entered the apartment building, I was welcomed by familiar smell of food: It was my mother's tomato sauce. I could distinguish its fragrance anywhere. It was a Thursday and it was pasta day.

Coming from a life spent on a farm, my mother's recipes were limited in number and not exotic. We had been bound to land and its traditions, and our eating habits had been dictated by the dependency of a self-sufficient farm: legumes, fresh vegetables, eggs, chicken, rabbits, pork, and fresh fruit. No, we did not come from a culture that did daily shopping.

In America habits changed in the way food reached the house, but the variety of meals changed only slightly. My mother became a daily shopper and continued to provide us, as much as possible, with the kind of food to which we were accustomed. She created delicious meals with simple dishes and simple ingredients. It was impossible to make tomato sauce with our own tomatoes, crusty bread with our flour baked in our wood oven, fresh ricotta from the milk of our sheep; but my mother shopped around for whatever came close to what we were used to eating. We never used supermarket packaged or frozen food. When we bought our own house, the adjacent garden was transformed in a productive vegetable garden, and it supplied us with all sorts of vegetables for six months a year. My father used to say that my mother could magically create a dinner by simply going in the garden. And she indeed had that miraculous ability.

In the kitchen my mother was also magic; everything was by experience, common sense, and intuition. Any recipe I remember of her cooking is vague to say the least: some sugar, some salt, some oil, and cooking until done. Her hands at the gas stove could estimate exact weight and precise cooking temperature and time.

In our family food was considered to be not only nourishment for the body, but for the mind and soul as well. Preparing meals was a domestic practice that bonded the entire family. Especially for special occasions my father liked to spend extravagantly to ensure proper feasting. The investment made sense to my immigrant parents because food was one of the few spheres in which they thought they could fully exercise power to hold the family together. Food was the glue that united us. It was at the table that domesticity, conviviality, respectability, and solidarity were cemented. Family food rituals like Sunday dinner created a distinctive domestic time and place where everyone, especially the young siblings, could act "Italian" and reaffirm their ethnic identity with no risk to the new public identities they were creating as Americans. Food was undeniably a recurrent expression of family unity and ethnic solidarity.

Food, the kitchen, and dining were also a celebration of the role of women in our family and community. My mother's kitchen was the center of the universe, a place where time and worries came to a sudden halt, remedied by the aroma of her baked breads, delicious *fagioli* and *patate* stew, marinara and ragù sauces, fresh chicken broth, with a handful of secret spices, a few squeezes of lemon and, of course, her magic touch.

After so many years I can still see myself watching as she grabbed and caressed ground lamb and parsley, chopped onions and peppers, her artistry undeniable. I especially enjoyed watching her making the ragù sauce, feeling its texture and consistency, inhaling the scent while it slowly cooked — just long enough until her nose signaled it was almost ready to make its debut on the table.

Her small kitchen was an island unto itself, a land of pure perfection. Her *panettone* and *pizza rustica* could bring joy to the heartbroken. Her chicken soup cured common colds, the heartier lentil rendition for a sundry of stubborn viruses. The simplicity of her spaghetti alla marinara brought calm to the beautiful chaos and confusion of grandchildren arriving at the front door. Scattering like ants, they awaited her summons to the tiny table where she dished out love-infused pasta and then surprised everyone with cookies and seasonal fruit. Even her cat wanted a piece of the action and didn't miss an opportunity to jump up, hopeful for a few scraps. Everyone — including the fearless feline, left the table in a visible and improved state of happiness.

I can't recall a time that I left her house empty-handed. She scavenged cardboard boxes and had a pantry full of containers — the Cool Whip, Ziploc, Pyrex varieties. Sending me off with at least a trio, she was quick to remind me to return them.

No matter what the mood or occasion, the tiny altar of her kitchen table, the sanctuary of a mother's gentle heart, offered comfort, respite, and soothing second to none.

Mothers nurture our souls. They feed our hopes and hurts. Her place in the kitchen reminds me how fortunate I was to have been raised in a house where no matter what the crisis or concern, the kitchen table, anchored by the woman who brought me into this world, remains a perfect sanctuary, and indeed, protection from "the wolves outside." Coming back from the IRS auditing that day her pasta alla marinara and chatter at the table brought me the soul nourishment I sorely needed.

NINE

Life for all of us had become a routine between work and school. The first ten months had not been easy. The uprooting, financial hardship, the search for a direction, the missing presence of my father who could have contributed to the family budget and, above all, provided guidance, had created an environment of uncertainty and fear. We were all working very hard and, at the same time, were determined to get an education, but the first objective was how to create a home where we could live decently. To the furniture and appliances that my grandparents had been able to put together for us, we had added a sofa bed and a washing machine. Having grown up on a farm with limited means, we did not have many desires and could easily find satisfaction in modest living. The experience of the war and postwar period had molded an outlook on life composed of simple joys and small gratifying expectations.

When my father arrived in July of the following year, the family was doing relatively well. Matilde and I were working during the day and going to school at night; the boys were going to school and scraping together some money with menial jobs. For them there was no time for sports, for Boy Scouts, or recreational activities.

My grandparents had succeeded in getting a visa for my father by soliciting the help of their lawyer, Mr. Eggart, who had a connection with United States Senator Kenneth Keating. The senator had taken our situation to heart and succeeded in obtaining a visa in ten months. While waiting, my father had sold the few animals we had on our farm and made arrangements with someone to take care of the land. He did not arrange a lease because he was afraid that it would have been difficult, with the new progressive laws, to take it back if he wanted.

We were all very happy that, after many years of psychological torture from an unjust denial of entry for political reasons, my father was finally in America and with us. He had never espoused a leftist ideology, never mind a revolutionary belief. He was a simple man for whom politics and ideologies were as foreign as "spirits" living on the moon. There was no reason to be resentful for the American mania of fearing political subversion from any individual that might raise a suspicion of leftist political inclination. What finally counted was that my father was with us to work together to build our long dreamed future in America. The ten months had felt more like ten years: My younger brothers and sisters had to learn to take the first steps in the new world without fatherly guidance and support. We had been pouring the foundation of a new life following our instincts and the role models we found around us. My grandparents, uncles, aunts and, above all, the Lonardo cousins were providing us with precious guidance to avoid missteps and pitfalls. Thanks to them, we weren't crushed by fears and anxieties.

My father was certainly very happy to be with us and, strangely, follow our footsteps. He was surprised to notice the progress we had made by ourselves and was anxious to become part of the mechanism to make the family function in unison. We all knew that it was not going to be easy for my father to begin an urban life, at his age, without skills and not knowing the language. My youngest brothers and sister Agnese in ten months were already able to carry on regular conversations in English. For my father, language communication was going to be a huge obstacle; indeed, it remained an obstacle for the rest of his life because in almost forty years he only learned a couple dozen words.

In a few days, my father started work in a plastic flower and toy factory with Uncle Attilio, Gianni's father. The factory was not far from our house and he could walk to work without any problem. It was an eight-hour job and did not require any special skills. Minimum wage was ninety-five cents an hour; *Papà* was earning a dollar. Working forty hours he would be bringing home forty dollars minus social security and tax deductions. Certainly it was not much, but it was going to make a difference in our family income.

However, we quickly sensed that my father was having problems in readjusting to the new work pattern in a factory, as well as to a new culture, and very different mode of life. For him uprooting was more traumatic. How do you transplant an old tree in new soil without damaging roots? My father had been willing to endure the trauma for the good of his children. At age 56 he was not dreaming of starting anew so that he could enjoy an easier life; but he was dreaming of a more promising future for his children.

One Friday evening, after he had been working at the toy factory for about two weeks, while we were sitting at supper, he started a long chat that threw our lives in turmoil. "The worst for someone like me and at my age," he said, "is to leave one's own home, where even the stones are one's friends, and when one's heart must break to leave them behind on the road." I immediately understood what he was saying or implying. It was painful at his age to think of the house where he was now living that was not his. I had read *I malavoglia*, by Giovanni Verga and remembered the drama of Padron 'Ntoni when the family lost the house that had been theirs for generations. "You are young; you don't know what it is," my father said; "you don't know, you don't know! When you can no longer sleep in your own bed, or see the light come in through your own window. I am old, and I know! — His own nest every bird likes best."

For nine months we had been working hard to create a new home for a new life. Eventually we were going to save enough money and would have bought our own house. Each of us had been doing his duty without grumbling; we had been waiting for the arrival of my father to strengthen the weekly pot of money that we were bringing home. I am sure that *Papà* had noticed that each of us had seriously assumed the heavy responsibility of family economy and, therefore, was not using that language because he had lost faith in our collective efforts to make it. Continuing in his melancholic tone he said, both to reassure us that we were on the right track, but also to reassure himself for what he was saying:

"I see that you are all good workers and don't shy away from responsibilities. And you know that in my life I have always worked like a mule, and was always confident to bring enough bread to the table for my eight children, and I prayed God to help me to do it as long as I lived, as my father and grandfather did it for their families. Blessed be their souls! Our mother, too, has done hers, and she has the same courage and determination as ever."

We were listening perplexed because of what he was saying, the affectionate tone he was using, but most strikingly, the amount of words he was using. My father was not very talkative. Whenever he spoke, words were measured and quickly conveyed a clear message. He came from an agrarian culture where beliefs were rooted in traditions and secular experiences and views of life were expressed through proverbs and mottos. Was my father preparing us for something?

"—No, my children, I am not what I was. Once, I was young and strong. The heart gets tired too, you see; it wears away little by little, like an old linen that has been washed too often."

I could not believe that was my father, the man I had watched all my life with thick calluses on both his hands working fifteen and sixteen hours a day under a scorching sun, in rain and snow, in freezing cold. I saw him once literally bleed from the bottoms of his feet, a man who had only a fifth-grade education and worked day and night to make it possible for his children to have the highest level of education they could achieve; a man who taught us all we needed to know about faith and hard work by the simple eloquence of his example. We learned about honesty and integrity from my father. And I learned about our obligation to each other from him and from my mother. Together they were able to build a family strongly rooted in the principle of dignity and now they were seeing their children go from a small farm in Southern Italy to become professionals. Their oldest son was already in medical school and momentum was with the rest of us to make it. And now, here we all were—in shock. Listening to him I was numb.

My father was not very old. He was not 56 yet, and was relatively healthy. He could not be surrendering because the job he had was too laborious. It just could not be. His past life on a farm, working the fields in adverse conditions without the use of machines, had been heavy. No, the work in the factory could not scare him. Could it be that for my father the house-temple of the patriarchal family we had in Italy was vanished?

The ethical values embodied by my father's old belief were not denied or mocked by our more modern view of life. We had full respect for the patriarchal family structure, which, despite its archaic features, remained for us a valid ethical model. If the values of work and abstinence were to be preserved in the new society, that task could be accomplished only by maintaining the internal cohesive force of the family, which could be threatened by the urban industrial society. The profound changes taking place in the economic sphere and the individualism of those who are attracted to it by the alluring possibilities of incredible economic growth tended to dissolve the extended-family structure.

Without knowing it, were we facing the struggle of reconstructing the internal unity of our family after only ten months of absence from my father? The Lonardos had done it and the family had been split for four years! The problem was more serious; it had to do with uprooting. It was a very serious trauma for my father. The Mignones had always been *padroni*. The land did not produce much but it guaranteed economic independence. And now, for the first time in many generations, the Mignones were not living under their own roof and were working for others. Was it possible that for my father it was difficult to accept a loss of social status? He was very attached to the ancient values and was struggling to maintain the moral integrity. It was not a matter of fighting an adverse "destiny." We did not lose our house in disgrace; we had given it up to move in a productive and social context where the prospects of progress were much higher. We felt confident that we were going to again have our own house and were again going to regain our social status and to achieve it, we did not have to engage in a fight against the course of history. It was not a matter of transgressing and questioning my father's wisdom. In America we needed only a will to work and the house-temple, the temple where the ideals of work and spiritual nourishment could be reconstructed again.

"I don't want to die on that job. I have done heavy work and I have done it in all kinds of conditions, rain, snow, fog, scorching sun, and I have never been afraid to endure the harshest conditions. However, I cannot continue to do what I am doing. Factory work is not for me. America is not for me. You have been able to settle well here, and God bless you. I will go back to Italy and finish my life on the farm on the Gran Potenza."

We were bewildered. Agnese, five years old now, started to cry. The rest of my brothers and sisters, astounded, were frozen. Dead silence prevailed. Nobody had the strength to say boo. We had been waiting anxiously for the arrival of my father to strengthen the moral and financial security of the family and, now in a flash, we saw everything collapse.

We had been noticing that my father could not sit straight and had been feeling terrible back pain. To cast off the state of bewilderment and break the tomb-like silence, I said, "*Papà*, you don't need to work at something that kills you. We have enough food for our table.... We can find something else that is not heavy and that you like. That job is not for you for sure." And we were able to learn about the heavy work that he had been doing.

He had been working near a machine that made toy guns to be sold at Christmas time. They were made of metal and, therefore, very heavy. I guess the popularity of the TV series *Bonanza* created a big demand for the guns. *Papà* was supposed to move the big container when full of guns, from the machine that was making them to another part of the plant. He could have used some type of chain crane to lift and move the garbage container, but he did not know how to operate it and was doing it by hand. Even the back of a Cyclope would have been in pieces at the end of the day. I was shocked that no one at the factory assisted him or showed him how to use the technology available. The foreman that was supervising the department was on the back of everyone and kept everyone moving. For my father, for the first time in his life, work had become a terrible way of living: endless and repetitious. Work had been deprived of its creative, gratifying function. It had become quantified labor. And having someone looking over his shoulder made it even more unbearable.

We finished eating and without saying anything, I left the apartment and went next door to talk to Aunt Flora. I explained to her that my father needed a new job, a different job. She thought for a short while and came up with a possibility to investigate. She knew someone at the church who worked at Mount Vernon Hospital; he was some kind of supervisor. With a determined voice she assured me that she was going to talk to him the very next day.

That evening I doubt that any of my brothers and sisters were able to fall asleep easily. How could they? I tossed and turned thinking about my father's tormented condition. We needed him more than he needed us, but his going back to Italy would have been an unhappy solution for him too. A return to Italy meant a defeat, and that was not part of our family, ever!

A new job, not a factory job, for the time being would be the solution.

The next day Aunt Flora came with a splendid solution. *Papà* was going to start work at Mount Vernon Hospital to take care of the grounds. We all agreed that that was the best blessing we could have hoped for. *Papà* was going to practically be a gardener; he was going to take care of flowers, bushes, trees, lawn, and no one was going to be watching over his shoulders. What was more perfect than that? He was practically using the same tools and doing the same work he had been doing in Italy with the advantage that he was assured a secure and fixed return at the end of the week.

Within three days, my father changed job and America became a happier and more hospitable land also for him, too. In the open air, my father could also continue to smoke his pipe, just the way he had done for all his adult life. He enjoyed especially taking care of the flowers. And the flowers in bloom, red, blue, yellow, spoke of my father's happiness. His supervisor once in a while stopped by to chat with him, proudly using his mixture of southern dialects. This was the beginning of what became a long family relationship with Mount Vernon Hospital and part of our family's realization of the American dream.

The work of groundskeeping stabilized my father's life in our family and in America. Work was pleasant, rewarding, and very fulfilling. At dinnertime we would get the report of the difference he was making at the hospital, especially for the flowers that he was caring for.

But when winter came and there was no more gardening to do, he was taken to do maintenance work inside the hospital. Breaking walls, changing flooring, painting, and anything else that was needed. Work again lost its appeal. It was not unbearable like work at the factory, but it was a burden.

One day at lunchtime, I decided to go to speak to Mr. Hertlein and ask him if there was a job for my father as a painter. In the basement of the factory there was a room where the exterior parts of the machines we built were painted. The father of the foreman was one of the two workers doing the job. George was just like my father: taciturn and reserved. Smoking his pipe, he painted and, where needed, with sandpaper and water, smoothed down the surface before giving the final spray of paint. I thought that would be a perfect job for my father.

Mr. Hertlein listened to my plea and gave the OK for my father to come to work. It was the perfect job for him. Although he and George could not communicate because of the language barrier, neither suffered isolation. My father had been used to working alone on the farm, and the new working situation did not create existential problems. And he was as happy as George to have his pipe and work at his own speed without having anyone looking constantly over his shoulders.

Every morning the two of us walked together to work and at times we had lunch together. However, most of the time I had lunch by myself because I was using that time to do part of my homework for the classes at night. My father understood how precious that time was for me and never came to my machine to share lunch. Looking back, I regret very much not having taken the time to chat with him and learn more about him and the past history of my family; I never had that chance again.

At the end of the day, at 6:30, my father went home and I took a ride from Joe for Roosevelt High School's classes in English. *Papà* continued to work at Hertlein until he retired. I believe that it was the semi-independence that he enjoyed in the basement of the factory that eased the transition from his mode of work on a farm to the pattern of work in a factory. The shock of transplant was mitigated by a fortunate combination of situations. The years that followed were some of the best years of his life.

My father never spoke of his experiences. He never boasted about anything. It wasn't in his nature. He always did it right and by the book. He was tough but fair. "Do it right the first time or not at all" was his motto. A man of few words, a quiet man. He spoke with purpose and honesty. When he spoke, he did not waste words; he did not need to, he led by example. His words were always measured. With everything he did, he made sure he gave it his best. He was a simple man who simply knew what was important in life and that view inspired us all and became our daily nourishment. Of all his accomplishments, he was most proud of his own family.

Having lived on a farm all his life he enjoyed working at his pace and having the freedom to decide what needed to be done. During the year he hired some day laborers to help him. He hired them because he could not do the work all by himself; tractors and other agricultural machines started to arrive in our area when we were about to leave for the United States. So all labor was done manually; and there was nothing romantic about working in those fields. The birds flew in the air and sang in a landscape that presented arresting natural beauty, but for the people who had to work in it in the rain, in cold temperature, or under a searing sun, that beauty could rarely be appreciated.

After the first months of adjustment, my father reasserted himself as the skipper. Always remaining planted in the old traditions and beliefs, he kept us anchored in the old moral values and work ethic. He certainly had not read *I Malavoglia*, by Giovanni Verga and therefore did not know anything about Master 'Ntoni, the patriarch of the Malavoglia family, but he acted and spoke like him. He too would lift his clenched fist, a fist made like a chunk of walnut, and say: "To pull an oar the five fingers must work together." And often he would add, "A family must work like the fingers of a hand: the thumb must act like a thumb, and the little finger must act like a little finger." And he got our family set out like the fingers of a hand. Each one of us assumed the role that would help the flow of the current of progress.

My father was very telegraphic in his messages; he liked to teach by the way *he* was taught: by action and proverbs. To encourage taking initiatives and giving advice, he would say "*Nisciuno è nato 'mparato*" (No one is born educated). To say that money draws the attention everyone, "*I soldi fannu veni' a vista 'a i' cecati.*"

"*Nisciuno fa' niente pe' senza niente.*" No one does anything for nothing.

"*Nisciuno te dice lavate 'a faccia accussi' si cchiu' bello 'e me.*" No one will tell you wash you face so that you look better than me.

"*Nun sputa' in alto che 'nfaccia te vene.*" Don't spit high in the air because it will fall on your face.

"*'U cane mozzeca sempe 'u strazzato.*" The dog always bites the poor.

Yes, he was a man short on words but not in deeds, and he led by example. While he did not have a college degree or even a high-school diploma by which to claim authority in a field, he probably had something better. We used to say that he had a PhD in common sense.

TEN

When I finally was able to enroll at City College as a non-matriculate in the evening division, it was like going back home. Not only did I know certain parts of the campus well, the club life, the social and ethnic composition of the students, but I also knew well how to maneuver through the labyrinthine academic and social life of the college. My previous experience had paved the way for me to move with ease and with a high degree of self-assurance. Since I was still working full-time at Hertlein Special Tool, I started CCNY by taking a few courses per semester.

Where do I begin? My life at City College began the day after the Harlem riots in 1964. Baskerville was still the chemistry building and I remember one day when the bomb squad came to remove an old bottle of a chemical that had become unstable. One lab was being remodeled and beneath the wood floors 300 lbs. of mercury was found. I remember taking swimming in winter at the Wingate Pool (bathing suits were forbidden) and then having to run to South Campus for my next class. I remember the antiwar rallies, the fight to preserve free tuition, Ravi Shankar's weekly concerts, and the Italian Club where I made the best friends I ever had. I remember Leadership Training and "T-Groups" that taught me so much about myself. I remember that my first-semester fees were $23 total. Most of all, I remember the education I received that was second to none and the respect I have had throughout my career when people find out I studied at City College. I am so happy that New York City has preserved some parts of the original campus so that future students can feel the presence of those who were there before them.

Similar to the friends that I had met with my cousin Gianni three years earlier, I was with thousands of immigrant children or children of immigrants, quite a few from Europe as consequence of being displaced by war. Many of them still carried emotional and psychological scars; others had suffered hunger or had strong memories of economic deprivation. We were seated next to young men who had come from different places in the world, but in one way or another, we had all been affected during our childhood by the experience of the war.

And there we were, together, with our diverse cultures but bound by some common experience. Our communality could be heard in the tone of our voices, in the determination with which we were pursuing our objectives, in the desire to be part of a society in transformation.

Being born into and having been raised in a large family of eight children, I learned about diversity early on in my life. Thanks to my brothers and sisters I learned what diversity means: We have the same father and the same mother but we are different one from another physically, psychologically, politically, and in every other way. Coming to America, we were not afraid to confront diversity. Differently from the Italian Americans we found, we did not fear the ghosts of the past and looked to the future with much curiosity.

In emigrating, which constitutes a second birth, one acquires a second life and will live with two lives, the second having a dimension determined by the age of the rebirth. My second life started at age twenty, when I was already mature and with a great deal of experience. I started to add new parts to my main identity, something American. In the American life, a new identity was built, brick over brick. It was shaped by new experience, encounters, sacrifices, sweat, patience, and passion. Going to City College, my life was reshaped in many ways. And so was the life of the friends I made there.

We happened to be at City College with a student body of unsurpassed brilliance and passion for learning that was disdainful of the "collegiate" preoccupations of other campuses. With a valiant but tiny and inexpert football squad, City did not offer a vigorous "collegiate" life to the nonaffluent, subway-riding city dwellers who eagerly pursued an education but were activated by a widespread militant radicalism in short supply elsewhere.

City College, as I lived it, was a place where the process of learning had a certain excitement and led to further learning, further growth. As in most colleges, surely for the majority of students, "learning" was only one activity among many, and not necessarily the "main thing," but at City the most exciting exchange and creation of ideas happened in the clubs, in the cafeteria, and especially in the rallies that very often took place on the lawn in front of Finley Center. The Harvard of Harlem had the largest number of students who, upon graduation, went on to pursue a PhD. Going to City College meant, for me, being a member of this group. It was a privileged experience, and I know of no one who participated in it who does look back on it with fondness.

As I arrived at CCNY, I became involved in the Italian Club where I met several Italian students who had recently emigrated from Italy. This group was slightly younger than the "clan" I had met three years before with my cousin Gianni but they were cut from the same stock; they all worked full-time, they all came from blue-collar families, and they all had the same strong motivation and the same strong drive to get an education and be successful. I met several young men with whom I remained friends for the rest of my life. With Vito De Simone I had a special bond. We were both about twenty-four and anxious to get through our degree as soon as possible. We had an equal appetite for learning and being committed to some social transformation. We both participated in the Italian Club and then the Student Government. I became President of the Club, Vito the Vice President. Due to my previous experience with my cousin's group I was able to get down to work with ease and more refinement.

The Pizza and Spaghetti Parties and Italian Nights became multiethnic events. By opening the doors of our events, we allowed the smell of tomato sauce to permeate the hallways of Finley Center and break down racial and ethnic barriers. Pizza, spaghetti, sfogliatelle, and cannoli brought in students from every walk of life and enabled them to appreciate Italian *gusto*.

The Club became a family affair. My mother prepared the sauce at home and my sisters along with cousins Clarice and Marisa, Gianni's sisters, assisted with the cooking and coordinated the dinner preparation. There were several girls in the Club ready to do the work, but my sisters and cousins needed a spotlight. My mother and Aunt Elvira gave their help for the events with the understanding that the girls would come along. In those years our sisters did not have outlets where they could meet men, and the Club offered unique opportunities for them to socialize and meet some nice fellows. Some of the girls saw my sisters' and cousins' presence as an invasion of their territory, but they couldn't make their feelings obvious.

I followed all the rituals that I had learned with Gianni: the first dish to the guards at the gate, special attention to Dr. Farmer, with due attention to the professors and special guests present. Because it was forbidden to bring wine, we would fill up empty Coca-Cola bottles with homemade red wine and pass it around to our special guests. "Dr. Farmer, how is the Italian coke?" "Good, very good; it's better than American Coke!" she would say. We contributed the homemade wine as a sign of affection but we also wanted to show off the skills of our parents: "Dr. Farmer, please taste some grape juice that my father made." I don't know if it was more benevolence or tolerance, but Dr. Farmer and the other guests went along with our shenanigans.

When we had pizza the preferred drink was beer and the camouflage was the use of ginger ale bottles filled with beer. It was fun, camaraderie, probably a small desire to break the rule. Dr. Farmer didn't have to worry about our behavior or our getting drunk. We were accustomed to wine at home since we were children and knew very well how to handle it. And in those years she did not have to worry that some crazy parent would sue her or the university for having allowed minors to touch alcohol. Students and recognized student organizations were not under the tight scrutiny of the Code for Student Conduct. I guess that's because there was more of a sense of individual responsibility; society was saner!

Students in the Club enjoyed each other's company and liked to socialize. Some encounters led to marriage; my sister Maria married Rocco. I must confess that while I recognized that it was important to take my sisters and cousins along, their coming with us imposed some restrictions on our conduct. Especially when there was dancing their presence hindered us from making passes at the girls with extra zest. Although Italian girls did not allow much play beyond the limits that preserved their "customary" appearance of purity, we liked the thrill of trying.

The openness of our Club activities had brought the Italian students in close contact with many of the students on campus and had given us a certain degree of popularity. Vito, who had been for a semester in the Student Council, had the courage to present himself as candidate for president of the Student Government. It was pure guts! The Italian students on campus constituted a small minority, and although we enjoyed the benevolence of quite a few students from other groups, especially the Jewish girls, it did not seem at all possible to win against a Jewish or even a Latino candidate. But Vito was determined to try.

Carolyn, his Irish girlfriend, became his strongest supporter and, in a sense, his campaign manager. She was incredibly organized and extremely determined. With an amazing amount of energy she launched the campaign with flyers that had slogans that could not be missed. The name of Vito De Simone was plastered all over the campus: on bulletin boards, entrance doors of buildings and offices, garbage cans, and on anyplace that could catch the attention of the students: "Vote Vito De Simone, the man with the clear vision for our future," "Vote Vito, the man with energy and passion to change the status quo." "Tell the College Administration that Students Want Radical Changes: Vito is our Man." "Join us, Students for Progress Through Quality and Free Education. De Simone is our Leader." Flyers were given out in the hallways of Finley Center and other parts of the campus. A few students from the Italian Club and a few Jewish and Latino girls lent their help. But our group was not big enough to do the work needed to elect the president of the Student Government. The other candidate, a Jewish student, had an army of people, well organized and with enough money to run a mayoral campaign. Although we were dwarfed by the magnitude of his campaign, I don't think that he matched the magnitude of our messages and messengers.

Carolyn, the general manager of the campaign, must have lost several pounds campaigning day and night. With her magnetic personality, always with a captivating smile, and conveying a sense of honesty and responsibility, she was able to engage people in short chats and deliver the flyers. She was worn out. Evening after evening of walking, making phone calls, writing letters, and planning events can take its toll on any campaigner's health and temperament. I don't know how she did it. It must have been true love. Indeed, Vito and Carolyn were married a couple of years later and are still together with the same love and loyalty for each other.

Although I had no time to spare, Vito was a good friend and I wanted to give my support; I also liked the thrill of campaigning. I tried to compensate for my rudimentary English with smiles and compliments to the ladies. It became a tremendous learning exercise. I quickly realized how people responded to optimism, determination, and an outgoing demeanor. All that was important, but our main concern was how to bring Vito to the people.

Vito had tremendous qualities: dynamic, amicable, and engaging, but he was handicapped by his still-limited knowledge of English and his English pronunciation. It was important for people to meet him and discover his personal qualities, but long public speeches were not the right platform for him. So we organized a well-orchestrated "Meet the Candidate" forum. In the ballroom, with a microphone in his hands and not standing beyond a podium but right in front of the students, Vito introduced himself briefly. We wanted to make sure that the students got a chance to see that Vito possessed the kind of personality to be trusted. Making sure that his natural, affable personality was still able to shine through even in overtime hours of tiring work was not easy. In addition there was the stress of the campaign. Vito spoke briefly about his life as an immigrant, although his was not exceptional in the context of City College, but it helped to connect well with the background of those students. Vito had arrived in the U.S. from Italy after an eight-year hiatus in Venezuela where he completed part of elementary and all of the middle school; therefore, he was fluent in Spanish. In the short introductory remarks he threw in, here and there, Spanish words: a well-studied strategy to connect with Latino students.

The forum was strategically planned to engage Vito in small talk, question-answer chat. Naturally, some of the questions came from friends and sympathizers, including several Jewish and Latino girls. Vito did very well thanks also to the choreographic work of Carolyn. He did not forget to refer to the previous popular president who was graduating that spring: "I will make every effort to honor his extraordinary legacy. And now, let's take the onward journey with vibrant energy and fresh perspectives." A couple of times we provided steam with a chant "Vi-to," "Vi-to," "Vi-to." Overall it was a good meeting and rally. Vito had given every indication that he was a man who takes the initiative, who is steadfast in his convictions, who dares, dreams, inspires, who kindles ideas.... but at the same time, humble. But elections are won on the basis of a secure number of supporters and our base was weak. The number of Italian students at City College was very low, and we were still carrying the stigma of the war, Fascism, the alliance with the Nazis, the horror of atrocities committed. We had established some strong friendships with Jewish students. But was that enough?

When election-day came, some of us took off from work a couple of hours earlier to help. And it did help: Some found a way to vote more than once. When the ballots were counted and Vito was named as the winner, we were incredulous at first. Was it possible that the impossible had happened? Was it possible that the "melting pot" rhetoric had peeled away differences, including prejudice, and voters had recognized our communality to aspiring and desiring a stronger homogeneous society and a new America? An Italian immigrant had been elected president of the Student Government at City College at a time when the campuses throughout the United States were becoming epicenters of social transformation!

The election of Vito made us feel as though we had been rehabilitated from an historic burden of chauvinism, bigotry, discrimination, injustice, and narrow-mindedness. The relief from that historic burden gave us a sense of freedom that was also felt as acceptance or welcoming to the larger social and cultural milieu. It was clearly evident that the aroma of our pizza, spaghetti with meatballs, and pepper and sausages, which had been attracting different students from the hallways of Finley Center was melting down boundaries of ethnic isolationism and reflected a softening of general consciousness toward the "other." It was probably this charged atmosphere that brought a new variety of students to the Italian Club activities.

In the Italian Club I enjoyed the collaboration of several students, but very often the old "clan" came back: Several of them were at Rutgers, where the Italian Club was nonexistent; others were already working. Their presence always created excitement and made the events a lot of fun.

When our cultural events ended early enough, very often, six or ten of us would go in a group to neighboring colleges and universities: Columbia University, NYU, Queens and Brooklyn Colleges. At times, we would proceed to Germantown in Manhattan looking for girls at various dance halls. At some of the dance halls there was an entrance fee; our first strategy of the evening was how to get in for free. We would knock our brains out to come up with a plan that worked. Once we had discovered it, it was applied over and over again. To enter for free in one of those local spots was part of the fun for the weekend. In retrospect, I don't understand why we were doing it. Yes, we didn't have much money to spare, but it seems to me that it was another challenge that we wanted to overcome.

One of the places we went was Lorelei. Italo was the ringleader: He was not particularly handsome, but he had a *faccia tosta*, he was *sfrontato*. He was a ball of fire. Uncontrollable. The rest of the group, mostly Southern Italians, was also lively but depended on his initiative and directives. In the group there were two men who were not Southerners: Ido, a Venetian, and Gerhard, a German, who was my close friend from Hertlein, my place of work. They both were very handsome. Of the two, Ido had a most captivating look, but unfortunately with a less dynamic personality. He was the "bait" in our fishing hunt.

At Lorelei there were a number of mature women, usually grouped together around the dancing floor waiting to be picked for a dance. Italo would make the round with one of us to assess the situation for the evening. Very discreetly he would make some comments: "This group is good; they are divorcees"; "These are too old, forget it;" "These are widows, not for us." "Italo how do you know that they are widows?" I asked confused. "Look at their faces," he said in a subdued way. "Oh, my God, they are like meat to be slaughtered," I thought.

We went back to our group and Italo gave the report. "There are some good chicks, but we must proceed with caution." We could not approach them as a group; it would have been an instant failure. Handsome Ido had to approach first, but with his flat personality would have collapsed if after a minute or so Gerhard or Italo didn't join him. And depending on the number of girls the rest of the group, one by one, would move in slowly. The technique was used over and over again.

Some of the guys were very good dancers, especially Gerhard and Giuseppe. My cousin Gianni, Rocco, and I were the worst. We could manage a Polka and some waltzes, but we preferred the slowest possible dances: We liked to feel the body of the woman while dancing! This very often created a problem for my cousin Gianni. "My pants are wet," he would confide, "I need a cover." Because this happened with a certain frequency, Gianni always wore a black or dark suit. But that too, would create laughs and entertainment. "Gianni, why did you have to squeeze that *fica* so hard? How many times do I have to tell you not to rub it against their legs," Italo would pontificate. "Gianni, that was a rock 'n' roll, you had to be jumping all over the floor instead of jumping over her body," Italo was continuing to amuse us. By the time we broke up to go home, inevitably we'd had had an enjoyable evening without spending much.

One time, Italo got along really well with one of the women on the dance floor and she allowed him to drive her home. The message arrived that someone had to take Giuseppe, his brother, home because Italo needed the car for a mission. The next day, a Saturday, phones were ringing all over with talk about Italo's adventure. Everyone had the story with some small variation but the ending was the same: Although the lady took him to her apartment, they did not end up in bed. The next time we met, Italo wanted to set the record straight, and he did.

When he entered the apartment he realized that the woman was well off. Her apartment, like the rest of the apartment complex was elegant: It was well-furnished and had some antique pieces that were really old. As he looked around, suddenly he noticed pictures of the lady with a man, the same man in every photo. Certainly he was not her brother or cousin, or a mere acquaintance. Some pictures revealed a close relationship, a loving relationship. Italo was confused. He did not know what to make of all that display of love of this woman for a man while he was thinking about having a nice couple of hours with her, probably on a king-size bed with the best mattress. He was baffled, mystified.

She saw his perplexity and tried to give him a knock: "You need a drink to relax, don't you?" "Yes, that would help," answered Italo while keeping his eyes on a picture of the lady embracing a man and kissing him. "Oh, don't worry, that's my husband," she said in a dismissive tone. That remark confused Italo even more. Was she still married and the husband was away? Away for the night? For the weekend? Working far away for a multinational? Or probably she was a widow who finally was enjoying some freedom after the death of a husband who had oppressed and repressed her? She could have also been a new divorcee and now was trying to breathe free air. He was looking for a sign that would confirm this last thought.

"Italo, come here, let's relax and tell me that love poem that you wanted to tell me on the dance floor." Somehow, all his emotions had been muted. He had driven her home thinking about what strategy to use to end up in bed and here he was without an appetite for anything. She took the initiative. "After a long abstinence, I would like a real taste of love," she said. On any other occasion, Italo would have caressed her with real tenderness, but that night he had a dilemma. The only way out of it. "Bella, could you tell me where your husband is?" he asked almost impatiently. "I told you, you don't have to worry about him; there is no chance that he will suddenly pop up. Impossible!" she said with a laugh taking another sip of scotch.

Italo was really becoming impatient. It was the first time that a woman had complete control of him. It was becoming a torment: He was the wounded mouse and the cat was playing with him. "OK, is he away working?" "Are you divorced?" "Is he dead?" he finally had the nerve to ask. "Yes, he is dead, and dead for good, and I must keep his picture around for my daughter, who was very attached to him," and she took another sip of scotch. That should have put Italo's mind to rest but it didn't work. While she was getting up to get another drink, the phone rang. It was incredible that she would receive a phone call so late a night. She answered and started talking, sometime with big laughs or irritating giggles. Italo got up from the couch and walked slowly around the room aiming for the door. The moment he reached the door, he opened it and left. We teased him and joked about the incident for many months. It had a big impact on us. Even now, so many years later, the memory is still fresh, and I still laugh.

A few times we wanted the experience of eating out. We chose to go to China Town in downtown Manhattan. To go to an Italian restaurant would have been a sacrilege: Weren't our mothers the best cooks around? Moreover, our pockets could afford only an economical dinner. The first time we went was a disaster. We did not know what to order; but worse, when we left, we were as hungry as when we entered the restaurant. Can you believe it: they did not serve bread? So, the next time we went, we brought a bag with Italian bread, which we kept hidden under the table. Once we were served, we started to pass the bag to each other so that each one could get a piece of bread. Inevitably the waiter realized it because breadcrumbs were all over the table. He called another waiter, probably the owner, and both spoke to us in Chinese. They were upset and not pleased with the mess. With incredulous faces, we were looking each other and did not say a thing. But Italo couldn't take the abuse any longer and decided to take the last piece of bread in the bag under the table and said: "It's bread." "What do you think it is, rusted ants?" And we left in good humor.

The "clan" remained active until the mid 1960s. For many years Giuseppe Battista organized a get-together, first at his house, and then at King Umberto restaurant where we still had a lot of fun, reminiscing about the time we spent together at City College.

My participation in the evening escapades lasted until I started to go to school full-time and switched jobs to work at night. My friend Nino Piscitello had seen an announcement posted for a night job and asked me if I was interested. It was a job for two computer operators, from 10 pm to 8 am. I did not know what a computer was, except for what I had seen in the movies or TV screens: big boxes with reels turning. I did not know how they worked, what they could do, and certainly, how to operate them. If it was a matter of pushing buttons, I could certainly learn.

Nino called for an interview, and off we went. The company, Diana Stores, was located in North Bergen, New Jersey, right across the Hudson. From City College, we went over the George Washington Bridge and arrived there in about ten minutes. It was a big, modern, clean-looking building. We entered through the main entrance and followed the directions to meet the supervisor, Sam, who greeted us with a big smile and a "Hello, guys." For us, immigrants, still not in full control of the language, that big smile was very reassuring. We sat, and he casually asked us a few personal questions: What we were studying? How difficult were the courses? When did we arrive in the United States? Whether we had come alone or with our families, etc. Still chatting, he told us that the job could be performed by one person, but the insurance and the fire department required that two people had to work together. In those years everybody smoked, and the specter of a possible fire made the ruling strictly enforced. "If you get the job, you will be the only one on the premises and the building will be locked with an alarm on. You will be allowed to open the outside door only in case of emergency." I was anxious to start the interview and to get it over with. Only years later, when I had an administrative job and conducted my own interviews, did I appreciate Sam's wonderful approach that created a relaxed atmosphere to break the ice and to relieve tension. Then, he proceeded to explain the job. Diana Stores Corp. had a chain of stores mainly in the Midwest, and sold mostly women's clothing. In those years, before the invention of the barcode, merchandise for sale had labels with tiny holes in them that bore the information for the article. Each article had two identical tickets. One of them was detached at the moment of sale and, in case of Diana Stores, these were mailed weekly to the headquarters in North Bergen. Sam proceeded to explain how the process of decoding worked. "But you don't have to worry about that because the process is done during the day. When you come at night you only have to deal with the reels." I was paying attention, but I did not understand everything. When he explained our work with the computer, I kept an eye on Nino: If Nino nodded with his head, I felt more confident and was reassured about our ability to do the work.

When he finished explaining the job—the sorting followed by the printing of reports—he asked if we felt confident in taking the job. Nino responded quickly conveying a sense of confidence. I also responded affirmatively, but with less conviction. Sam registered my response and without missing a beat said, "And, of course, we will train you for a month." "For a month?" I replied incredulously. "And naturally you will get paid," he added. He had understood that I could not afford giving up a month without pay. What an incredible man and what a country, I thought. They will teach me and they will pay me! Yes, what a country, I thought again.

Sam called Walter, the man who was going to be our direct supervisor, he introduced us and told Walter to take us to the computers and give us more of an insight into the work. Walter was young, about thirty, easy-going, and very jovial. His mother was Italian American and he was dating a black girl. Times were certainly changing! There was no more tension: We got the job and we were going to be able to do it well.

Since Diana Stores was not far from the George Washington Bridge, it was possible to take classes during the day and in the evening. We just had to find the time to sleep. But super-smart Nino made life easy. We divided the work in two stages: sorting and printing. Sorting was the job that required skills; printing required monitoring the printer: there was a slight possibility that the paper would jam. Nino did the sorting and I did the printing, two operations that took approximately the same amount of time.

We quickly came to the conclusion that it would have been a waste of time for both of us stay awake all night, so we decided that while Nino did the sorting I would sleep, and vice versa. We would collect the desk chairs that were flat and line them up to make a bed. With the plan that we worked out, each of us could sleep four hours. Thinking back, I don't know how we were able to sleep on those bumpy chairs, but probably in those years we could have slept on rocks.

The work was easy and not too demanding. A couple of times I messed up. It was easy to fall asleep just watching the printer do its job. Once I fell asleep and must have slept for a couple of hours because the paper in the printer had jammed and had ruined a couple of hours work. We did not know what to do. We did not know if there was a way to ask the computer to restart the printing from the point the reports being printed were ruined. So, we decided to call Walter. It was a stressful situation because it was about four in the morning, but we didn't have an alternative. Walter did not complain about being awakened but did not give encouraging solutions: "You must restart the printing from the beginning." This constituted a big problem because we would not have had the reports ready by 8 when we finished working and the day employees came to pick them up.

Nino was truly disturbed by the fact that Walter did not give us a solution. He was convinced that in the working logic of the computer there had to be a way to tell the computer to start the printing at a certain point. The lack of a solution for that incident truly troubled him. After a few months, I messed up again, this time I had fallen asleep around six. This was a real problem because there was no way we could have the reports ready by restarting the printing at 6. I woke Nino up and with embarrassment told him that I had messed up again. Nino shook his head to wake up faster and went to one of the machines where cards for the program were punched. In those years computer programs consisted of information punched on cards. He had been fooling around with the machine occasionally, but I never paid attention to what it was that he was trying to do. He punched a card and fed the information to the computer. The reels started to turn fast, after a while they slowed down and the printer started to print. We checked the report: The printing had started from the point that it was ruined! We both jumped into the air and our screams were probably heard all over North Bergen. Nino had discovered how to tell the computer where to start printing. This meant that if I screwed up again, it was not a big tragedy.

Nino was majoring in physics and had an incredible logical mind. He became very interested in computers, and while still at Diana Stores he created a computer program to monitor sales for their liquor stores. Not bad for a guy that had been hired to do elementary jobs. Well, when Nino graduated, he went to work for a bank in New York as an informational technology operator. In later years, he became the Vice President of a big bank in charge of all computer operations.

Diana Stores offered us a big change and in my case a colossal change. I was not working anymore in a factory and going to school with hands stained with motor oil and smelling of burned oil and metal. I also had great flexibility in arranging my class schedule. As a full-time student, I was taking some courses in the evening before going to work, and some courses in the morning, after work. I would go home around 10:30, get some sleep, and do some studying. It was stressful because of the night work and because I had only limited time to study.

While taking day courses at City College I met a new bunch of students, most of them five or six years younger than I, children of Italian immigrants who had arrived in America in their teens and had done most of their high school years here. Although their English was good because of it, they had a strong Italian identity. This is the period when I met Mike Nigro, Michele Pesce, Pasquale Perretta, Rocco Galatiotto, Tony Negovetti, the Criscuolo twins, Vincenzo Bollettino, Bob Bongiorno, Franco De Luca, Romeo De Rose, Dominick Salvatore, Pietro Sia, and many others. It was a lively group that had more free time available to benefit from the college experience.

Occasionally, but very rarely, I would go to the Italian Club office and meet some of them. The club office was very small and consequently was jammed during certain times of the day. When the weather was good, some of the guys would play soccer on the lawn in front of Finley Center. Mike Pesce and Mike Nigro were two big stars. One can only imagine the smell in that club office when they came back from playing, especially in warmer days!

But the club was also a love refuge for occasional escapes. The doors had two panes of glass, but the men had covered them with Italian posters to promote Italian culture! One of the guys had donated a used couch to the club to improve the ambience and make it cozier. And, indeed, it made the stay in the office more comfortable for various activities!

During the day there was also a clan that stuck together, mostly going to the cafeteria or walking through Finley Student Center.

They had a passion for teasing girls, especially the Latino and Jewish girls. Since most of them were studying Spanish, the Italian group enjoyed practicing it with the girls.

"Ciao, Juanita, como estas hoy?"

"Yo no soy Juanita; Soy Rosita."

"O, sì, Rosita la bonita." "Un beso para mi prima Rosita la bonita" and he would throw her a kiss.

The names would change, but the approach was the same. The guys had come up with the idea that Hispanics were their cultural cousins and were also searching for the open door to American cultural diversity.

Martin Luther King had already made the famous speech "I have a dream," and we were in the middle of the civil rights struggle. The need for true equality for all black people had made a big impact on all of us. Some of us participated in national and local demonstrations organized to strengthen their social, economic, educational, and political rights. Italian immigrants and most Italian Americans also took that message personally as a need to correct an historic and consistent general abuse of many people who were considered second-class citizens, including Italian Americans. Our young Italian immigrants believed that they would have prospered more living in a nation proud of its citizens, regardless of their color or ethnic origin. The friendly approach, therefore, used by the Italian guys also carried this message.

The Italian clan of the day club, like the evening group, wasn't big, but was very noticeable. It had energy, vitality, and zest. They could be annoying, but they were mostly enjoyable and pleasant.

They would not hang around with Italian girls or make passes because the girls would not go for that kid stuff. They were too shrewd and too disarming. With half a sentence they would put us flat on the floor. A couple of guys wanted to be phony with them and were put down in a way that everybody got to know it:

"*Va da mamma che ti dà il bibero'!*" Go to mommy, she will give you a pacifier!

Even more insulting from another girl: "*Va' da mamma che ti dà la mammilla!*" Go to mommy, she will breastfeed you!"

Several of the guys became university professors. Dominick Salvatore became an international authority as an economist and was a consultant for many banks and finance institutions. The Criscuolos became businessmen in restaurants and pizzerias. Pasquale Perretta, after earning a PhD, gave up university teaching to become a big real estate investor.

Vito continued to be a court interpreter. With his native knowledge of Spanish and Italian, including southern dialects, he became a well-respected interpreter for the federal courts. For extra money, he worked at night and on weekends transcribing and translating taped phone conversations from FBI wiretaps. It was interesting work that provided him with practically a second stipend. He never revealed the content of the tapped phone conversations, but one time he made a remark about how easy it was to decode the language used by drug dealers. After listening to two or three phone conversations, sometimes in a mixture of Neapolitan, Calabrese, and Sicilian dialects, it was easy to connect the dots. He went to Italy in his role of official interpreter of the American Justice system for the Michele Sindona case, the bankers who caused the collapse of the Franklin National Bank.

Some years later, when my daughter Elizabeth became an Assistant District Attorney, we went to see my City College friend Mike Pesce, who had become the Administrative Judge of the Second Judicial District in Brooklyn. He had informed security that he was expecting us. When we arrived to the court building, they allowed us to park in a reserved parking spot of the court and were escorted to his office. We went to the top floor of the court to Mike's office and were greeted royally. It was an emotional meeting. Looking over the East River toward Manhattan, imaginatively toward City College in Harlem, we reminisced about our experience at City College and blessed America for the opportunity we were given.

"Mike, did you ever think, while we were at City College, that you were going to become the chief judge of this court?" "No, and I never dreamed that so many guys of that group were going to be so successful." We talked and talked to savor our journeys. Mike continued his success to become the Presiding Justice of the New York Supreme Court, Appellate Division for the 2nd and 11th Judicial Districts. I don't know if City College still produces exceptional leaders from the working class at the rate of those years.

ELEVEN

In 1963, less than three years after we arrived, we moved into our own house. A five-apartment building had gone up for sale on Penfield Street, exactly behind where we were living. My parents acted quickly on the purchase: one street away, in the same neighborhood, and very close to my grandparents. It was a giant step in our lives. By buying the building, we would not be living in a rented house anymore. For my father it ended his depression: The Mignones could claim their secular status—living in their own home. It was a great deal for all of us; but it was of bloody importance to my father.

In less than three years we had succeeded in putting down fifty percent of the cost of the building, and for the rest we took a mortgage. Certainly it was not what my father had been dreaming; "the Mignones never had debts," he used to say, but at least for now we were living under our own roof.

How did we succeed? By functioning like a beehive where individuality and self-motivation were put to use for the common good of the family. By going to school, each one was pursuing his or her own future and simultaneously our work contributed to the advancement of the family. We worked to help support my brother in medical school in Italy and to build the financial base to buy a house for our family's security. We did it through our combined efforts, the efforts of the entire colony with my mother as queen.

I had always known that my mother was an incredible woman, but when we came to America I had a full sense of how great she had been and how strong she was. I knew that she had endured the loss of her first three children when they were still toddlers and that she had had two miscarriages. I also knew that she assumed a heavy responsibility running a household of ten people and helping with chores on the farm. But now, in America, she was assuming responsibility for care of the entire family on every level: She was the wife and the mother, the cook and the family banker, the dreamer and our spiritual leader. She was a supreme mother, an exceptional wife, an extraordinary sister and aunt, and later on, a remarkable grandmother. She was part of a generation of giants who could build anything from nothing, part of that generation of Southern Italian immigrants who arrived in this country rich only in hope, faith, determination, and an unrelenting desire to see their children better off than they were.

When my mother married in 1931, at the age of 17, she entered a family with five brothers-in-law. In those years, any woman would have had a difficult time coping in a similar situation. Not my mother. She quickly earned the love and respect of everyone and became the queen of the Mignone family. Everyone sought her advice and good judgment. Her brothers-in-law went to her for advice on anything; they even sought her opinion on the women they were going to marry. She had eleven children and, although she lost the first three at a very young age, she never allowed the scars of their loss to affect her role as a loving mother for the rest of her eight children. She had the strength, the courage, and determination to provide love, affection, dedication, wisdom, and leadership for the family. Even after she had enabled us to become doctors, dentists, professors, and schoolteachers and after we had married, she remained our most trusted advisor, counselor, and sustainer. She was always so full of resources, solutions, and alternatives. And because of her dedication, determination, and fortitude, we became more than we had aspired to be.

The fact that my mother had only a third-grade education did not prevent her from becoming our mentor even in school matters. In our early years in school, while living in the farmhouse, at night, while we were studying, with the excuse of knitting or mending our clothes, she would sit at the table and keep us company. Inevitably she would memorize with us an assigned poem, be it in Italian, Latin, or Greek. When we were at the university, she knew exactly when each of us had an exam and made her concerns felt and her trust in our abilities. With a large soul and a humble heart she lived and died at the service of her children. Who knows how many candles she burned for our exams? We could open a store if we would put them together! As we received our diplomas, as a symbolic gesture, we hung them in her living room, and they became the trophies of her victories. When she died many years later, in the early 1990s, I had the honor of delivering the eulogy. I was shaken by her sudden death, but my feelings of admiration were unshaken. In concluding the eulogy, I remember saying this:

Although you had very limited resources, you did not accept limits for your children, and you succeeded because of the power of your moral values, the strength of your unshakable faith, the depth of your determination. You knew that family warmth and security had no substitutes; they could only be created, not bought or borrowed. You nourished us with that supreme gift of love throughout your life: from those early years when, all together, we would say the rosary around the fireplace, to these later years, when we would often get together around a table for a Sunday dinner that you had prepared for all of us, your presence retained that magical power of uniting and nourishing us morally and spiritually. The love that you gave to your children was then extended, with the same intensity, to your sons-and daughters-in-law, grandchildren, brothers and sisters. When we got married, sons and daughters became immediately your sons and daughters. Each one was special to you: who was married to your oldest son, who was married to your youngest daughter, who was your first daughter-in-law, who was your first son-in-law; it seems that each one was first for you, and each had special virtues. If one of us would ever hint something negative about one of them, we were definitively wrong and we would go home with the conviction of being wrong. And what about your grandchildren? They were the coronation of fulfillment of your desires. Although you had 28 grandchildren, the high number did not make them lose a special place in your heart. You knew by heart the birth date of each one of them and, inevitably, the morning of their birthday, you were the first to call. For them too, you were a reassuring force.

Everyone has a mother and most of us have or have had great mothers. In our families, we all had exceptional, extraordinary mothers. My grandmother, Aunt Elvira, Aunt Italia, Aunt Flora, were all exceptional women. To a great extent, we may say that we are what we are and we are where we are because of our mothers. It doesn't matter how much we appreciate and value what they did for us, we cannot usually call all of them matriarchs. In our case, we were surrounded by an incredible group of matriarchs.

A woman becomes a matriarch through a combination of circumstances and qualities. To be at the top of *"un Casato,"* of a set of families of the same lineage, is the result of many combinations. It takes a special individual to be a matriarch. That person has to have the instincts of nurturing, the aura of knowledge and wisdom, and the patience to be the mother of many offspring. It takes years to fortify this role. Years of being where you are needed, solving crises and being the mother within the family circle to whom everyone looks up, can trust, and from whom they feel safety. Those fuzzy feelings are not the only important ones, but the feelings of authority and identification of being a disciplinarian must exude from a matriarch. True matriarchs don't have to work at having these qualities. They just earn them. Those qualities are crystal clear and sometimes very powerful, as most people under them often seek out the shelter, comfort, and yes, discipline of that person who can give them advice, solace, and unfiltered sound common sense. The hardest thing for matriarchs to do is negotiate not stepping on the toes of the mothers of children who are not her own.

Our matriarchs were extraordinary women for their wisdom, love, and commitment to the family. Shrewd observers of people, they understood more about human nature, and what people might do or say, than most psychologists, but their gift is their ability to radiate a motherly presence to anybody from any walk of life, let alone their own families. They were fearless in their ability to say exactly what was on their mind and in such a manner that people did not feel threatened, and their willingness to talk about any subject was admirable. They understood that life is for living and that there was no subject that could not be discussed, because information was important, and how information was obtained was even more important. Our matriarchs preferred topics of morality and religion, the history of the family. We loved to hear their strong voice of morality. Each and every member of the family knows of events, and can tell a story of how their presence and actions affected his or her life.

That is what matriarchs do. They rule not by threats or power, or money. They rule by love, and honesty and trust. They were feisty, forthright, and sometimes too tough in their views, but it was never mean-spirited. You always knew that at the core of what they were saying was love and your best interests. The lessons that I learned from our matriarchs are invaluable lessons that one could never ever learn in a school. Their nurturing, discipline, wisdom, provided me with a more solid foundation than I could ever have hoped for. These were people of integrity, honesty, loving, and dignified personalities, who came from nothing, and valued everything for which they worked. They wasted nothing and never bought things just to have them.

I feel completely fortunate to have had these extraordinary matriarchs. My mother and her sisters believed that just about everything was "God's will." "*È la volontà di Dio*" slipped off her tongue frequently, no matter how terrible or trivial life's twists and turns. If someone died, it was God's will. If there was a drought, flood, deluge, any natural calamity, my mother declared it God's will. If thousands of people died in a famine for which they failed to prepare, God's hand was at work. She also believed fervently in the power of prayer to shape God's will. With a strong faith she nourished her life and those around her. The phrases, "*È la volontà di Dio*" or "*Se Dio vuole*," found their ways into our vocabulary as well, like a melody you can't get out of your head. It was Mamma's credo in "God's will" and her deep faith and observance that gave her strength and saved her from succumbing to her sorrows. Her apartment, especially the bedroom, was like a sanctuary: prayer books and rosary beads on the night table, and pictures, carvings, or statuettes of Jesus, Mary, Joseph, and an assortment of saints on every wall and flat surface.

The most striking picture in my parents' bedroom was a life-sized image of the Sacred Heart. It dominated the wall where the dresser was. Candles, a flickering light, and fresh flowers from our garden in summertime, completed the picture of the shrine-like setting. It was like the bedroom of my other relatives. My grandparents' and my Aunt Elvira's had the same array of saints and Madonnas; the only difference was which saint had the spotlight. They all professed religion with the same intensity and passion, the only difference was who was chosen patron saint or the major religious interlocutor. Religion also took the little spare time my mother had.

Whenever she could, together with her sister Elvira, she would go to the church to be involved in a couple of societies.

Our family had been a practicing Catholic family and had been attached to the Church for generations. Especially my mother's side of the family had always practiced religion and had been strongly connected with their local church. The church was a house of worship but was also a place where the ladies of our families could practice and display their social skills. They believed that they had special organizational skills and higher common sense. Unquestionably, they did.

Like most Italian immigrants, my family continued to profess religion in America the way they did in Italy. Its practice was unquestionably one of the most relevant definers of my family and of Italian American ethnic identity. It was so also for historic reasons—after all, the Catholic Church has its roots and base in Italy and has molded the life and consciousness of Italians for centuries. But Italians, especially Southern Italians, for centuries have tailored Catholic beliefs to their own individual needs.

For my family and for most Southern Italians, living in an agrarian economic structure and culture where the state was absent and people lived on and from the land at the mercy of mother nature, religious belief in the supernatural forces that controlled drought, floods, hail storms, and any natural cataclysm was a natural option. Guided by the Church, people lived with hope in a world pervaded by danger and uncertainties. Religion offered belief in the efficacy of magic and devotion to saints and Madonnas, along with a basic indifference to and distrust of government. When people needed help for their crops or a miraculous cure for themselves or members of their family or protection from dangers, both seen and unseen, they appealed to their favorite Madonna or saint. The saints, having been human and enjoying a special position in Paradise close to God, enjoyed special devotions and love in the hearts of the people.

My mother and her family, along with the Italians who emigrated, brought with them a strong and realistic sense of religion, professed with fervor and an irrepressible expressiveness. In America too, their faith was guided by an innate urge to externalize and materialize spiritual impulses in art, architecture, and elaborate ceremonies, which clashed mightily with the religious practices of both Protestants and other Catholics. Moreover there is a rich tradition of piety centered in the privacy of their homes. Pictures of saints and crucifixes decorated homes: Votive candles flickered before homemade shrines of saints, the Virgin Mary and Christ (well portrayed in an interesting and revealing movie, *Household Saints*, 1993, by Nancy Savoca). Saints and Madonnas were (and to a certain extent still are) worshipped in a variety of ways through many social contexts, both inside and outside the walls of the churches, in streets and squares. The rhythms of family life followed the liturgical calendar, with appropriate foods prepared and prayers said for the feast days of important saints. A private religious life was complemented by public *festas*.

In essence, Italian American Catholicism, both pragmatic and worldly, lacked any "surrender" to the transcendent; it was a Catholicism mediated through vehicles, which were personal, concrete, immediate, and situational. Thus, it is not surprising that Italian Catholicism clashed with the religious practice of other Catholics, especially the Irish who controlled the hierarchy of the Catholic Church in America. When the Italians came to America the external and exuberant religious practices clashed with the reserved and private Anglo- and Irish-American practices. The Irish-American Catholics viewed the public festivals, processions, and pageants in honor of various saints and Madonnas as flamboyant paganization of true Christianity. They did not have the cultural predisposition to accept that the "civil" part of the *festa* was mere amusement, an occasion to show collective love and gratitude to a saint or Madonna; and that food, music, and companionship were a public expression of joy and thankfulness for the "protector."

Nevertheless, the Italian immigrants added their own unique contributions of warmth and spiritual fervor. Most importantly, they contributed money, labor, and creative skills in consolidating the presence of the Catholic Church in America. Thousands of churches, Catholic schools, hospitals, and mutual aid societies were built with labor and the contributions of Italian immigrants. Italian priests, friars, missionaries, and nuns came to America in large numbers to assist and to guide. A special religious order, the

Scalabrinians, was specifically created (1888) with the aim of caring for the spiritual and social welfare of immigrants. Mother Cabrini became a leading personality in the American Catholic Church by creating many schools, orphanages, hospitals, and places of social assistance.

For my family and for most immigrants, the Church played an extremely important role as the unifying link between the old and new world through the continuation of various religious celebrations. The presence of priests who spoke the immigrant's language helped to solidify the Italian community and cement old traditions. Ethnic parishes bearing the names of patron saints of the *paesi* left behind were important cultural bridges between that world the immigrants had left behind and the one that their children were participating in building.

Saints and Madonnas were worshipped through many social contexts, both inside and outside the walls of the churches, in streets and squares in a variety of ways. In our Southern culture, the veneration of saints and Madonnas was imbued with a high dose of paganism. Sacred images were often seen with such superstitious symbols as *il corno* (twisted horn), worn to ward off *il malocchio* (the evil eye); rituals were performed to ward off the evil spirits. Although there were some who might eschew the *corno* in favor of the scapular, the cross, or the religious medal, often it was possible to see Italians wearing a combination of secular and religious items.

In our culture, both the cult of the saints and the cult of Mary were more popular than the cult of Jesus Christ. In part, this is the result of a sustained belief that the saints and the Madonna are more accessible and receptive to human needs. We related only marginally to Jesus Christ. With the exception of Christ child adoration (which also features the grieving Madonna), Jesus was generally seen as too abstract a figure to correlate with everyday existence. Michelangelo, with his Pietà, focusing on the grieving mother, reinforces this popular belief.

In our Southern culture, an extraordinary number of religious rituals revolve around the Madonna where she is one of the principal religious forces in the life of the people. Southern Italy's strong attachment to the Madonna is related to the matriarchal character of its peasant society. Historically, Southern Italian mothers have played focal familial and social roles; popular veneration of the mother of Christ is a natural phenomenon there. In the eyes of many, Mary is the strongest advocate for petitioners, for she alone can plead their cases directly to her son, the God-made-man Christ. She is called upon for her capacities to grant favors and perform miracles. Of course, there is only one mother of Christ, but for Italians, the Madonna has many identities and titles, which differ, based on her numerous abilities and her special relations with people in various locales. Hence, distinctive devotions call upon her specific titles and attributes.

The popular religiosity of many saints, which include allegiance to saints of particular regions, is another characteristic of Italian Catholicism. Saints are models of a perfect life to be emulated and, because of their ideal life, they enjoy a special relationship with Jesus and God and therefore may act as intermediaries for those who ask for help and spiritual guidance.

In our town we celebrated several feasts in honor of our patron saint. Madonna delle Grazie, Sant'Anna, and San Leucio were the biggest. People came together for a shared celebration and commemoration of our village and city patron. On the feast day, the saint or the Madonna was honored through all manners of rituals, as family, friends, and *paesani* skipped everyday activities to demonstrate their individual and group devotion. Though it was a religious event, the essence of the *festa* was its merging of the sacred and the secular ("religious" and "civil") programs of activities. Among the activities were a procession in honor of the saint, the carrying of lighted candles as a sign of devotion, and the recitation of prayers. Even the Italian men, whose socialization fostered resistance to more formalized aspects of Catholicism, were happy to immerse themselves in feast activities and express devotion to the saint in the process. Year after year, at various intervals during the year, the *feste* served as a periodic divergence from the monotonous routine imposed by work and as a mechanism to reconnect us collectively to Church and faith.

We participated actively. My mother took part in the processions, many times holding a burning candle in devotion of the Madonna, and often would take some of us with her. Many mothers would take their children in the votive march that would become a manifestation of devotion and of imploration. This spirit permeated life as a whole.

I believe that that strong faith sustained my mother in all her daily activities and made our life at Penfield Street harmonious and secure. The rental of four apartments and the money that each one of us was bringing to my mother was quickly creating a condition of financial stability. Although we had managed without a car for three years, we were able to afford one. Uncle Gaetano gave us his old Buick Roadmaster that he used to pick us up at the airport. The huge car could easily seat seven people. I had already passed the road test by practicing with my cousin Gianni's Ford and was able to assist the family when needed. Soon Matilde obtained her license and became the second driver in the family.

In three years, we had practically achieved the status of average Americans: a family car and living in our own house. Probably we had more than the average American family. We were collecting rent on four apartments! But what was more reassuring was the fact that we felt very confident in moving up the education ladder. In fact we were all in school. My older brother was moving through medical school in Italy, I was at City College, Matilde had enrolled part-time at Fordham University, Maria was starting Lehman College, Nino and Biagio were doing very well in high school, Domenico was in junior high and was editor of his school's newspaper, and Agnese was in Mt. Carmel Elementary school.

Pride was important for all of us, and for some, more than others. For my sister Matilde pride was connected with appearance. She had found it too demeaning to work in a dress factory and invested a lot of time and family pull to find a job that carried some prestige. After two years in America, speaking an English that was far from perfect, she found a job teaching kindergarten at Our Lady of Victory in Mt. Vernon. Most likely she was making less than what she was making in the dress factory, but she felt gratified and delighted by the position she was occupying. She probably also did not want work at a job that was beneath the occupation of her Lonardo cousin who was a kindergarten teacher at another school in Mt Vernon, Mt. Carmel Elementary.

Pride and appearance became determining factors when Matilde started college. All of us, including the Lonardo cousins, made CUNY our educational system to realize the American dream. Not for Matilde. She chose to go to Fordham where she spent on tuition practically what she was making as a kindergarten teacher. And as a kindergarten teacher she paid her way for a PhD at New York University. The rest of the siblings, with the exception of Domenico, who went to Cornell, made City College, Hunter College, and Lehman College their paths to success. Each had been able to combine work and school.

In retrospect I don't know how we managed: seven of us, sixteen years apart from the oldest to the youngest, at the same time, attending school and working. Matilde, Maria, and I had to devote the first few years to learning English and started college part-time in the evening. The boys were thrown in school without knowing a word of English and, after the first few months of terrible frustration, started to progress in their studies and gradually excelled. Nino, seven years younger than I, arrived at City College in my last year there. Biagio, ten years younger than I, skipped two grades and enrolled in City College as I left for graduate school at Rutgers University.

It was not an easy life. Yes, the family was united, but we saw each other only briefly at night and on weekends. Mamma was the linking rod. When we had a bite to eat, at different times, Mamma connected the dots of the family and informed us about how everyone was doing. She would stay up until the last one of us came home and sit at the table chatting and sharing family information. Probably our children and grandchildren will find this hard to believe, that each of us had such high a sense of responsibility that our parents never had to stimulate, motivate, or encourage us to do more. Many years later, when I was already married, Mamma once confided to me that she felt pain in her stomach those times that she had to wake me to go to work. I had told her that in case I did not get up by 6:45 to wake me up. She was the one carrying on her shoulders our stress and our *stanchezza*.

Sunday was a time for family reconnection. It was the day that we dressed up to go to Mass and had the time to eat and laugh together. My brother Nino inevitably had something funny to relate that had happened either at work or at school. Invariably the boys would tease each other. My mother would rejoice to see her family complete for a rite that unfortunately took place only once a week.

My father was the silent observer. When we were in Italy, dinnertime was when he reprimanded us and gave us some terrifying admonishments. A few times, I can still remember as if it were yesterday, he said, "If you don't want to study, no problem, you will go to be a servant for Uncle Egidio: In his condition, he needs someone to assist him around." As a boy, Uncle Egidio had lost one of his hands in a shotgun explosion and the family assured him a future by allowing him to pursue a degree. This led him to become principal of a junior high school; as such, he could have afforded a servant. He was the only member of my father's family to have a college education and was always perceived as someone special, in spite of being physically handicapped. Although he loved us, I don't think he appreciated the fact that my father had given life to so many kids without having the means to provide us with a basic livelihood.

Uncle Egidio had a strong sense of irony; at times, it was very pungent. On the occasion of Agnese's birth, the last of the eight siblings, I remember Uncle Egidio telling my father: "Bravo, and now you also have someone to provide you with bread for your old age." But my father who had self-control and a sharp memory too, said, "You never know, I might need it." When my sister Agnese started working at a bakery while going to school and brought home *leftover* bread, many times while eating it my father said, almost as vengeance, "My youngest daughter is bringing home the bread as my brother foretold. The Lord is great and powerful."

In America, after the first couple of years of adjustment, my father mellowed and became more appreciative of his children, even though he almost never made complimentary remarks on our behalf. He was superstitious and I think he was afraid of the *malocchio*.

TWELVE

We had become part of mainstream America. Not only did we have a chicken in the pot and a car in the garage; we also had a house. Having "our own roof over our heads" we had regained the sense of security that we had growing up in Italy. The house-temple provided us with a home base and the social status that my father lamented that we had lost. We needed a house to provide the family's very roots and unity, as a source of comfort, nourishment, and self-awareness. It was also needed to restore the honor of the family. We had conformed to the old logic of sacrifice carried over from life on the farm. The refrain that the Mignones had always been *padroni* had helped to stimulate us to regain lost status.

Coming to urban America it was not easy to continue to use the same economic structure or approach to life on a farm. The IRS agent drilled me during an audit on the fact that I had insisted that the paychecks from work went directly to my mother, the cashier of our household. "You give the entire check to your mother?" I remember him asking with insistence and astonishment. Everyone had been contributing to the meager finances of the family. Everyone had been pitching into the family treasury with the same passion and the same conscious effort. Everyone was taken by anxiety, but no one was destroyed by his or her unbridled and untimely aspirations. My father had succeeded with his example of relentless efforts to create *benessere* for his family to sweat and toil endlessly for the progress of the family. What became so unique about my family was that everyone accepted that ancient way of thinking. There was no transgression of the traditional laws of work and self-discipline. By remaining faithful to our established values and struggling to maintain our moral integrity we were rewarded in that no one brought dishonor to the family.

There is no question that the objectives were reached only by maintaining the internal cohesiveness of the family, which could have been threatened by individualism in the face of all the alluring possibilities of the new. No one fell by the wayside; no one wanted to be doomed. No one ostracized himself or herself from the family. The struggle for survival turned first into a struggle for progress and then into a collective effort to realize one's own ambitions.

Our home had become an anthill of vitality: Everyone was making a contribution while pursuing his own individual future. I had graduated from City College and had moved on to graduate school at Rutgers University in New Brunswick to pursue a PhD on an NDEA fellowship provide by the federal government. I had found Paradise on earth. I could not believe that I was getting paid to study. It was a big change in my life. For the first time I did not have to do any physical work. What a country! It was an unbelievable situation. It took a while for me to be convinced that it was moral to get paid just for studying. No one in my family had had that experience: to be paid for one's own intellectual and cultural enrichment and to pursue one's own future. It was such a new situation for me and for my family that if I wasted a few hours without studying, I had the feeling that I was cheating someone.

By going to Rutgers I had followed in the footsteps of my cousin Gianni, my future brother-in-law Rocco, my good friends Giuseppe and Italo Battista, and the Sclafani brothers. For us immigrants, Rutgers was our second discovery of America. City College had offered to us, children of blue-collar workers, the possibility to jump on the escalator to social mobility, but it was Rutgers that would take us to a professional life. Most of us had done our undergraduate studies while working, sometimes full-time. Regardless of how driven we were to learn, the time for studying was very limited, and for the most part we only succeeded in doing what was minimally required. It was in graduate school, holding either teaching assistantships or fellowships, that we could immerse ourselves in study.

Unquestionably, I felt that I had reached graduate school academically and intellectually handicapped. Having had to work, I did not have time to enjoy the life of the campus: the lectures, concerts, movies, socializing with friends and classmates discussing intellectual issues or probing new ideas. My time had been split between work and classes, and only what was left over could be for studying. But when we arrived at graduate school we had the time to catch up and we did it by working very hard.

Our experience may help to answer a few questions about immigration. What happens when farmers migrate to industrial cities? And how does immigration affect a family's relationships, both within the family and outside of it?

It is clear that when we came to the United States we did not suffer any alienating effect. The relationship between modernity and tradition is neither dichotomous nor linear but dialectical. Our family managed well in the move from the rural to the urban industrial-service environment. Urbanization, immigration, and industrialization don't always have the same impact on people. In our case, operating traditionally in a modern society was the best way to move forward collectively. Our family was flexible, and while adapting to new social conditions, continued to rely upon traditional forms and ways of forming relationships. In a situation with a variety of options we adapted our Old World ways accordingly. Some old modes matched the situation; other did not. Those that did match were retained more easily. We had found a more stratified and anonymous society, and pressures that could have produced family instability were considerable. Tradition—familial or otherwise—interpenetrates and facilitates social changes and makes economic progress possible in that it continues to satisfy basic human needs, even in modernizing societies. We were very prepared for the change from rural life to industrial-service work patterns. Certainly, it was not a smooth transition for my father who had worked all his life on his land and came to America when he was almost fifty-six years old. Some difficulties and conflict occurred, but not disorganization and certainly not desertion. The traditional nuclear family pattern proved extraordinarily resilient. Right alongside our nuclear family, the extended family also survived and helped in the adjustment to the New World.

Notwithstanding work pressure and the anxiety created by the course load in school, we managed to remain close as a family. Nino as a biology major at City College was on his way to graduation while working on weekends in a drugstore at 241st and White Plains Road. Biagio had graduated from high school when he was not even 17 years old and was financing college at City College as a biology major by enrolling in ROTC. Domenico, in high school, had become active in clubs and was dreaming of spending his life in the public sector. The boys had considerable aspirations for the future and my mother was dreaming with them, but a latent concern was the lack of financial means. We had been managing to get through undergraduate studies without overwhelming financial problems. Thanks to CUNY, even children with very limited financial resources could earn a degree and become part of mainstream America.

The first big change came when Domenico started to talk about going to college away from home. My oldest brother, Enrico, was forced to go away from home when he decided to study medicine. There was no university in Benevento so there was no other choice. He went to Genoa, quite a distance from Benevento, but in an emergency my Aunt Italia lived in nearby Savona. In fact, many times, on Sunday he would go over for dinner in order to spend time with that part of our family.

However, Domenico wanted to go away, possibly to an Ivy League school. When he was accepted at Cornell with a substantial scholarship and decided to go, my parents went into a state of depression. As the youngest boy of the family, he was always perceived as a boy and now the young boy wanted to leave the family. I remember the day that we took the trip to Ithaca. I was already teaching at Stony Brook University and my mother called to ask if I could help him move with my station wagon.

We left very early in the morning for the long ride to Ithaca. Halfway, we stopped at a rest area and had lunch. My mother had prepared a frittata sandwich and had added some fruit in the sandwich bag. It had been a somber ride with no one speaking. Domenico must have been concerned about his separation from home and the unknown waiting for him. He had never been away from home and now suddenly he would be living on his own. In a sense, he was as fortunate as my oldest brother, Enrico, because he would be able to attend college without having to hold a job. His scholarship was taking care of the tuition; my parents were going to take care of room and board. The problem was cutting the umbilical cord. My mother had been silent because she could not swallow the bitter pill of seeing her son leave home. She wondered if he would ever go back to the Bronx after graduation.

Just before arriving at Ithaca, we stopped again to have another sandwich; it was prosciutto and provolone with fruit. It was a more talkative stop. My mother repeated once again the advice and warnings that she had been giving for a while. Mostly she was telling her youngest son to eat well, to dress warmly in winter, not to get wet in the rain, and to be careful about the friends that he was going to choose. "*Chi va con lo zoppo incomincia a zoppicare,*" she repeated once more. "If you sleep with dogs you'll wake up with fleas." Knowing how talkative and argumentative my brother was, I limited my advice as not to waste too much time with clubs and social events.

When we arrived at the Cornell campus, we asked for direction to his dormitory and with help here and there, we arrived at our destination. There was a bunch of cars in front of the building and families were unloading suitcases, boxes, containers, and all sorts of things, even bicycles, small televisions, and stereo systems. Some were unloading onto carts and in groups, helping the students to move in. I quickly realized that those kids were from well-to-do families and wondered how my brother was going to mix or to survive, in a student body composed of students that had money. I started to worry how Domenico would manage when his friends went out to eat frequently or invited him to go to the movies and he did not have money. I was wondering if it wouldn't have been better for him to go to City College as all of us had done and not feel embarrassed for not being able to be socially active.

We had a long trip to get back home and could not waste time. We took the only two plastic bags of belongings from the car, put them on the curb, kissed my brother and left, with no further ceremony. Years later, when my wife and I took our oldest daughter, Pamela, to college at the University of Pennsylvania, my second time helping move, I thought about that trip to Cornell. Now our station wagon was full with boxes tied on top of the roof. When we arrived at the student residence we unloaded our daughter's belongings on a cart and took several trips to the room that had been assigned to her. I parked the car in a parking lot and went back to the room. My wife and Pamela had already found a system to organize all the clothing. I did not know how to help so I sat on the bed and relaxed. When it was time to hang some pictures, I did my part and the room began to feel warm and look pleasant. "Not bad for a dormitory room," I thought. "Before leaving, let's all have a bite to eat," my wife said.

I was not talking. I was thinking about the trip we took to Cornell. The sandwiches, the two black plastic bags left at the curb, and my brother standing there in a sea of people helping to move their kids in, helping to decorate their rooms and then going out to dinner. When we took that trip we just did not understand that aspect of collegiate culture; it was not just a matter of money. We had never been exposed to that ritual. I don't know how my brother felt or what he thought, but we were unaware — just unaware.

By 1970, of the eight siblings, my brother Enrico and I were the only two who had completed our studies. Nino had developed a strong interest in dentistry, which had to be sustained by financial means. But something of the American saying "where there is will there is a way" pervaded the culture of our family, and it seemed to have been created just for us. Nino could not afford to apply to many dental schools and he could not afford to live away. He applied only to those dental schools to which he could commute. As usual, my mother was always encouraging, mostly relying on her strong and profound religious faith. I don't know how many candles she burned. When Nino was accepted to NYU dental school it was perceived as something almost inevitable. "I knew that he was going to be accepted, the Madonna had to do this grace for us," she said confidently.

Nino managed well. While going to dental school, he worked on Friday evenings, Saturdays, and Sundays at the drug store. It was not an easy life to balance, but being at home provided the usual security with physical and spiritual nourishment. Furthermore, he did not have to cook, wash his clothes, or clean his apartment. Certainly, he did not have the time to socialize or go to movies or sport events. Today we would say that it was dull and lacked excitement.

About a year later, it was Biagio's turn to apply to graduate school. His dream was to go to medical school, and he had been enrolled in ROTC since he started his studies at City College. The ROTC provided him with enough money to go through college without holding a job, and he graduated when he was barely twenty. He did very well because he was very systematic in whatever he did. He had an extraordinary ability to concentrate and a special ability to synthesize information. I am sure that if he had decided to pursue graduate studies in science, especially biology, he would have been awarded a fellowship or at least a teaching assistantship. But his dream was medicine.

Biagio was a very conscientious young man to the extent that he was too realistic. ROTC was going to provide him the means to pursue medical school in exchange for three years of service upon graduation, but he was too concerned about not being accepted because of a lack of extracurricular activities and not having any "special" connections. Yes, he did well in his courses, but he was not the type to lick the feet of professors to get strong letters of recommendation.

One evening, while eating with my mother seated in front of him for company as was her custom with all of us, Biagio revealed to her his plan for medical school: "Mamma, I am not going to apply to any university in our area because I will be competing with too many students, and many of them will have strong support." "What?" she said, "You want to go away? Are you crazy? You are a very good student and you will have no problem?" Biagio did not want to waste money in applications since he had very limited resources, and he tried to explain again to my mother that applying to New York's schools was just a waste of money: "Mamma, you don't understand. You don't know how the system works. You just don't know the culture. Do you want me to become a doctor? If you want me to become a doctor I have to apply and hope to be accepted at a school in the South where I have some chances. Don't worry, when I finish I will come back to New York."

My mother was tortured by the idea of her son leaving. Toward the end of supper, regaining her sense of hope, she told my brother to go ahead with the applications to the schools he had planned but insisted that he apply to at least one school in New

York with a promise that she would pay the application fee. I don't know how many times she went to church to burn candles and how many rosaries she must have said. On the occasion of a feast at Our Lady of Mt. Carmel, our church, she also had the audacity to speak to the bishop about her son applying to New York Medical College, which was a Catholic medical school. My mother spoke a broken English, but most of the bishops and cardinals speak Italian, and I must assume that my mother made a passionate and warm appeal. Nothing could stop my mother, not even the language barrier.

Biagio was accepted by several medical schools, including the sole New York school to which he had applied at my mother's insistence. And so that is where he pursued his medical degree. My mother was a person who highly valued gratitude. Biagio would probably have been accepted without any intervention of human or supernatural power; my mother provided my brother a strong sense of security.

By the time Domenico graduated from Cornell, the family had broken through many barriers. My father had only a fifth-grade education, and my mother a third-grade, but by the beginning of the 1970s there were already two physicians, a dentist, and two PhDs teaching at the university level among their children. And the rest were on their way to forging their own paths.

Domenico had gone to Cornell with the intention of pursuing a degree in Political Science so as to go to law school. My parents, especially my father, always dreamed of having a lawyer in the family, almost as much as a doctor. My father had bad childhood memories of how some terrible and dishonest lawyers freed a neighbor who stole two goats from my grandfather. But the composition of the family quickly changed and medicine became the dominant profession among us. Domenico decided to pursue medicine, too. Not having enough courses in science, he enrolled again in college for a year, this time at Wagner College in Staten Island.

Medical school had become expensive in this country, while in Italy it was still practically free. With the help of my brother Enrico who had graduated from the University of Genoa, Domenico enrolled there. With Enrico's mentorship and constant advice, Domenico was destined to become the third physician of the family. I don't think that when my brother Enrico enrolled in medical school he ever thought that he was going to start a family tradition, and that within a span of ten or twelve years, he would be followed by nine other doctors from our family, between brothers and first cousins.

We had been a small part of the real secret of the phenomenal success of America's genius of human capital. Thanks to far sighted private and public investments made in the United States throughout the nineteenth and twentieth centuries, the vast majority of Americans—across lines of class, gender, religion, national origin, even race—attained levels of human capital higher than those found in any other nation. The overwhelming success of our nation is that a majority of its citizens, and not just a privileged elite, possess high levels of human capital put to productive use. Living in a society rich in human capital also confers benefits on the community as a whole.

Education is the single most important determinant of any person's or group's human capital. There is tangible empirical evidence that a country's human capital is largely proportional to the educational attainment of its adult population. If immigrants have less education or fewer skills, the country still gains valuable human capital because immigrants generally possess a more robust work ethic than native workers. In addition, immigrants generally arrive with strong family ties, and strong families generate higher levels of human capital in the next generation.

Our story also shows that immigration has been America's most singular human-capital advantage. We have always admitted far more immigrants and integrated them more thoroughly than any other country on the globe. Our experience has molded a belief in the greatness of the United States. We are not only the freest people on earth, but also the most dynamic because of the constant flow of immigrants. We are never content with the status quo; we are always looking to improve ourselves—both as individuals and collectively—and generally we succeed in doing so. There is a definite link between the socioeconomic characteristics of a region and the living arrangements found within a nation, region, or ethnic group.

My family certainly is clear evidence of these observations. If we look at the success of the Asians in our country, we must definitively point out that it is due to the high energy that they bring to America, which immigrants possess in general—but also by their strong family unit. The Asian family structure must be considered as probably one principle-determining factor of their success.

America had been good to us. With hard work we were climbing the ladder fast. Family unity had been a big factor. There was a dynamic process of give and take between new conditions and old social structures. Normally Italian families experience low rates of dissolution probably because of this innate necessity to stick together. Family stability grows from family consensus. If extended family ties limited the Italian family in general occupational achievement by restricting us to the local community, kinship structures were also adaptable to our immediate needs. As an important economic unit, chief socializing agent, and tradition's custodian, kinship structure had its own power to inhibit, counter, or adapt to a variety of social pressures. The price that we paid was limited occupational mobility.

THIRTEEN

By the mid-70s I had settled at Stony Brook University and my sisters were already teaching in different schools, with Matilde testing the grounds at different local colleges. The boys had realized their dreams: Nino a dentist, Biagio an ophthalmologist, and Domenico an obstetrician. They had followed the path of our oldest brother Enrico who had shown that the children of farmers could become doctors, very good doctors. The courage of Enrico was not only exceptional as the first in our family to enter the world of medicine, but he was the only son of a farmer in our area to challenge the old order and aspire to what farmers perceived as a most noble and prestigious profession. Yet more courageous was his decision not to stay in Italy after graduation but to come to the United States to join us. He did not know English, and he had to take a very difficult multiple-choice exam in order to apply for residency and internship in an American hospital. However, he did come, he faced obstacles and monumental difficulties, and he overcame them.

What made life less painful and stressful and probably stopped him in moments of great frustration from going back to Italy was not so much his family but the woman whom he eventually married and with whom he created an extraordinary family. I think he met her a few months after his arrival here in 1968. He married her two years later. Their entire relationship was based on Enrico's passing the ECFMG exam. He had taken the exam once prior to their meeting. At that time he had to look at his neighbor's exam because he didn't even know what "first name" — and "last name" meant in English — he did not pass the exam, but he passed the English section!

To begin to earn some money and to set foot in an American hospital he started working at the Italian Hospital where he did the pension medical/physical checkups for the Italian Consulate in New York City. He received $50.00 a week.

When Sheila and Enrico met, Sheila did not speak Italian and my brother did not speak English; it was a perfect symbiosis for learning each other's language. While Sheila was in Ecuador, Enrico wrote her a letter in which she picked out the word *cuore* — she figured "heart" and that he loved her — he was telling her about *Zio*Vincenzo's heart attack and the meaning of *cuore* got defined!

My brother found out that there were prep courses for the ECFMG; he took the course at St. Barnabas in Livingston, N.J. The two of them, in love by now, went together to class so that Sheila could take notes on the lectures and he could focus on the content. It was rather difficult when the lecturer called on Sheila with a question believing that, as everyone else, she was enrolled in the course! Unquestionably the symbiosis helped to strengthen their love relationship and improve my brother's English, but it did not accomplish the main objective. When Enrico took the exam a second time, he still did not pass. Their disappointment and frustrations were enormous.

So, then my brother began to literally copy the medical books — English on one side, translation on the other. He stayed home, read, studied, copied — and he passed the exam on the third try. That was life-changing for him and Sheila and they married that spring, but it was also a big turning point in our family.

Why didn't my brother give up and go back to Italy? Family and pride played an important role. For an emigrant to go back to his village as a failure can be catastrophic, even more so for someone educated. But Sheila played a determining role in his endurance.

Their wedding certainly cemented Enrico's determination to stay in the United States, but it also showed how fast we were moving up the social ladder. Several dignitaries, including the Italian Consul General in New York Vieri Traxler along with the Director of the Italian Cultural Institute, the Cardillos, and the two Vice Consuls, Agostino Mattis and GianFranco Cosenza, attended the wedding. This was the first of many occasions to come that ambassadors, consuls general, judges, and other personalities would attend Enrico and Sheila's social events.

Now married, Enrico carried out his internship and residency at the French and Polyclinic Hospital on West 50th St. and became chief resident in Internal Medicine. Throughout this time my brother constantly called Sheila day and night to get a translation into Spanish (as well as a translation of all the dirty words in English that were being bounced around the emergency room). Their first apartment in the city consisted of one room with two sofas. Every night they had to put the two sofas together and then crawl in from the bottom—it was like sleeping in a crib! But it didn't matter much since Roberto, their first child, was born during that first year! They graduated to a larger one-room apartment, and by the time they had three children they had a one-bedroom apartment—Roberto slept on the couch, Laura slept in the crib, and John slept in the baby carriage.

At Christmas, that first year, they invited Sheila's parents, my parents and brothers and sisters, and the interns and residents without family. They had a full-size Christmas tree in the one room and a long table. In the middle of dinner, one of the doctors was called out on an emergency at the hospital, and we all had to get up and leave the apartment so that the doctor could get out!

When they moved to White Plains, Enrico took a course in English at the Adult Education division at Rochambeau School in White Plains. However, by that point he was working as chief of the medical clinic at the Polyclinic, beginning a private practice, and still doing the pensions for the Consulate, so he had little time to systematically learn English. Sheila was probably more of a detriment than a help because he would presume she would do his homework a half hour prior to class!

When they finally moved to Bronxville, it was the first time they had their own bed (the previous furniture was all hospital furniture). The first night they were so excited about finally having their own bed—they tried to put it together but the side slats did not slide correctly and they ended up sleeping on the floor! But life was good and getting better fast.

Their house in Bronxville, a big Tudor on almost two acres, was the gathering place for many family and social events. It was a reflection of our entire family's success and a symbol of our pride. When special guests were invited, brothers and sister were also asked to join them and socialize. We were given the opportunity to rub shoulders with "the big ones." We had succeeded in making the adjustment, progressing in a few years from living in a farmhouse in Southern Italy to sharing food with prominent guests of the family in one of the most affluent areas of New York.

Enrico, as the oldest, had truly provided inspiration and paved the way for the rest of the family. As part of his strategy to find and attract patients, he opened his office on the ground floor of our home on Penfield Street. It unquestionably gave my parents a huge sense of pride seeing the sign indicating the medical office of their son in front of the house that had been bought with such sacrifice.

My mother and Sheila both played a role in building the practice. Sheila had given up her teaching profession—she was teaching Spanish at Fordham University when she met my brother—to become my brother's primary assistant. She was not just the answering service and the secretary; she was the manager and promoter in the office. She had learned Italian and was able to court the Italian immigrants in the area that my mother was feeding into the office. After the Italian Mass at Mt. Carmel Church in Mt. Vernon and during any social event my mother would find a way to pass out my brother's business card. She had an extraordinary way of connecting with people, and they, in turn, responded to her smooth and cordial demeanor. She always amazed me with her communication skills, clarity of ideas, and, above all, perseverance.

Enrico soon shared the office, enlarged by another room, with Nino. Nino hung his name below Enrico's, and the two Mignone brothers offered medical and dental service to people in neighborhood and to friends that my mother channeled their way. I am sure that my parents would have loved to see hanging outside their building the names of their other two medical sons also. In fact, my father had offered them offices in another apartment of their building; it would have been the Mignone Medical Center offering family medicine, obstetric, ophthalmology, and dentistry!

Nevertheless, the four brothers did succeed in opening medical and dental offices in the same medical center in Yonkers. Looking at the directory upon entering the building, it was an incredible sense of pride for my parents every time they went for a checkup to see the names of four of their sons.

Because of the size of the family and the wide network of friends my brothers built a very strong practice in a very short time. Their knowledge of Italian and the ties with the Italian Consulate without any question contributed to the success. All of us had good health insurance and could have gone to any doctor; but there was a sense of pride walking into their offices as a member of the family. Sometimes we would go on off hours or whenever we needed assistance. When I was a child my biggest fear was that my father would get sick. There was no health care then and affording doctors and medicine could be financially difficult. And here we were, doctors at our convenience.

When people asked my parents how they managed to create so many doctors and professors, my father would raise his shoulders and say "È stata la volontà di Dio." There is no question that it was God's will, but there must have been also personal determination. My parents literally lived for the good of their children, and many times I wondered how they could endure so much sacrifice practically for their entire lives. But then, I don't think that their sacrifices carried pain because they gave of themselves in a natural, instinctive way. When today students tell me that their parents, who make a rather good salary, are not able to pay for their education, I become depressed: We are living in a sad culture. Some of these parents go out to eat two or three times a week but cannot afford to support their children. Some students declare themselves to be independent from their parents so that they can milk Uncle Sam.

We did not come to America to beg for alms from Uncle Sam. My family, coming from a farm, had always lived relying completely and exclusively from work. In my father's view a lazy person is like an abandoned dog. Consequently, we firmly believed in the gift of willpower that God had given to us and made the best use of it. Work is not just a sacred right, but it is also the best realization of ourselves; it reflects who we are.

I noticed that my brothers had chosen professions that gave them a high degree of independence in their work. They had their own office, set their own work schedule, and opened their offices wherever they wanted. They were in full control of both time and the workplace. It was probably in their genes, part of their inheritance from farm culture.

My nephew Roberto reminded me when he opened his own hedge fund that "*Nonno* said that the Mignones never worked for anybody."

The family was evolving and progress was becoming more tangible. My mother, always motivated by her religious belief, reminded us not to be blinded by shining gold. "No one lives from bread alone," she reminded us often. And we remained attached to our religious faith. Sunday was the traditional day of going to church and having dinner at home.

Family values certainly were the strongest factors also determining our marriages. We were not aiming for a marriage to get rich or to seek easy success. Before starting a serious relationship with someone we had met, our parents asked us and we asked ourselves what their family was like and what kind of family values they had. I certainly made my choice based on who my wife was; but the person she became was the result of a certain upbringing and family values. After I met my in-laws and spoke with them a few times, I realized that my family had a lot in common with them, especially on issues dealing with family.

My siblings did the same thing. Regardless of ethnicity, their spouses and their families were family-centered. Their in-laws, regardless of their occupations, never considered the wellbeing of the family a secondary priority. To a great extent, the success of our families was also molded by our spouses.

As we married, the family branched out in subunits. I had settled on Long Island close to the university where I was teaching. My brother Enrico settled in Bronxville, and so did Nino and Domenico when they each got married. The three brothers bought their houses within a half-mile radius of each other. My sisters also settled in Westchester within five miles of each other. My brother Biagio, who wanted to have horses and goats and needed land, was still in Westchester. Except for me in Stony Brook, my seven siblings settled in Westchester, between ten to twenty minutes from my parents.

My brother Enrico's house became the epicenter of activities as the family grew in size. It was at his house that my youngest sister's wedding was celebrated. And it was at his house that we had social events of importance. As the oldest of the family, Enrico assumed a role of leadership, and Sheila seconded him in that. Their house on Sunnybrook Road became the place to encounter friends and personalities of various political and religious classes. Ambassadors, consuls, senators, congressmen, bishops, monsignors, and businesspeople very often were guests for dinners and receptions. The family was invited to meet and mingle. My parents, if it was a gathering of those who spoke Italian, were also present. At one of the first events, I remember my mother scolding my father for the way he was dressed. "What's the matter with you, why didn't you wear the suit and the blue tie? Your sons are doctors and professors and you still dress like a farmer."

Mamma's scolding must have had a big impact on my father. From then on he dressed up on Sunday and every time there was an important event. My brother and I bought him another suit with a vest. And that became his outfit for special occasions. He added a nice watch-chain to his vest and a handkerchief in the breast pocket of his jacket and became a *signore*. My father had always dressed with decorum and spoke with kindness; but now he presented the image of being "someone." Even my mother appreciated the new look and jokingly said, "You are not looking for another woman, are you?"

My father and my mother were very frugal and rarely splurged. Before the family got too big with grandchildren and we were able to all eat together, it was the time to indulge. My father rarely did food shopping, but when he did, it was noticed; he always bought the best of everything, especially fruit. Another big splurge was the trip to Italy. He loved to bring back *torrone* and the customary bottle of *strega* liquor. In one of his last trips, after my mother had died, he did something heroic. While he was there, he asked his sister-in-law to take him to her jewelry store because he wanted to buy a couple sets of earrings. My aunt did not ask questions and away they went.

Having arrived in the store, when their turn to be waited upon came, the clerk asked him: "Yes, uncle, what can I do for you?" "I would like to buy a couple pairs of earrings," my father said softly and a bit timidly. "What do you mean a couple pair? How many pairs, two, three?" the clerk said in a hurry. "Well, I need seventeen pairs," my father responded. Incredulously the clerk asked, "Did you win a lottery?" "No, it's better than a lottery; when I go home there will be seventeen granddaughters waiting for me," my father said in a strong voice. Mystified by the answer the clerk said, "You are right, it must be better than winning a lottery."

Indeed, when my father came back, every granddaughter went to say hello and received her pair of earrings. I don't know if each of them was delighted by the design or shape of her earrings, but I am sure they were touched by that sign of affection from their grandfather. I know that the grandchildren have already started to pass those earrings down to their children and the legend goes on of how my father stunned the jeweler when he bought them.

By the early 1990s, the family was flying as a unit. We had all been married for a while; we all had good jobs and children. My mother had started to raise grandchildren. Some of my siblings, especially my sisters, because they were working, dropped off their children at my mother's and went to work. When I occasionally passed by mother's apartment, it looked like a day-care center. Being over seventy, it was not easy for her to deal with so many children, but she had the courage to endure pressure and labor. It was unquestionably a labor of love.

When she unexpectedly passed away in Mt. Vernon Hospital because of bronchitis, her loss was felt strongly by every generation of the family. Children, grandchildren, and in-laws felt the same pain. She was so proud of everyone and all were so very proud of her. The day before her sudden death, I had gone to see her. She regained all her energy and pride when the nurse came to check her: "This is my son. He has a PhD, is professor and chairman of his department," she said with delight. "Oh, wow, you really have a great family," said the nurse. "I have three doctors, a dentist, two university professors with PhD, and two teachers," said my mother with some emphasis on each of them. I was somewhat embarrassed. But there was no arrogance in that list and in her voice. Suddenly I remembered the story of Cornelia and her sons Tiberius and Caius Gracchi, which we had heard many times in our elementary school as an extraordinary example of pride and nobility of spirit. Soon after the death of Cornelia's husband, the Egyptian monarch Ptolemy VIII Physcon proposed but she refused him outright in order to remain faithful to the memory of her husband. She was praised for her devotion to her household and the education of her children. Cicero states that her children were nourished more by her conversation than her breast. At a time when other women of her age openly displayed ornaments, Cornelia declared that her sons were her most precious jewels. One day, a rich lady, proud of her jewels and her wealth, came to visit Cornelia. Cornelia listened quietly as her guest told her of the precious stones and ornaments she possessed. When at length the lady grew tired of talking of her own beautiful things, she said she would like to see the treasures of her hostess. So Cornelia led the lady to another room where in bed and fast asleep, lay her children. Pointing to the little ones, she said to the bewildered visitor, "These are my jewels; the only ones of which I am proud."

For a woman like my mother who had to stop formal education at the third grade and had devoted all her life to the family and to the education of her children, the degrees earned by her children became the trophies of her victories. With purpose, when we received our diplomas, we hung them in her living room. It was not an arrogant act to display our achievements; it was an expression of gratitude to our parents for the enormous sacrifices they had chosen to endure for the good of their children. And there they all were, about twenty diplomas, practically taking up an entire wall as a tribute to our parents.

When my mother died in 1992, at age seventy-eight, she was savoring the fruits of her extraordinary work. It was Easter Sunday morning, and we were hoping that she would be released so that we could spend the day all together. Instead we spent the day planning her funeral.

Death and misfortune had been around and remained present in the background of our daily lives. Roberto, the first son of my brother Nino, was born with some physical problems and we, as a family, were shaken up by it. We had to endure another of nature's setbacks when Richard, my brother Biagio's son, was born. Biagio and his wife Kathy did everything possible to give a normal or close to normal life to their son. Richard went through two liver transplants and did not reach age ten before he passed away. It was a loss that left a big scar especially in the consciousness of his siblings and deep pain in the heart of his young cousins.

Then, in 1993, my brother Enrico was diagnosed with gastric cancer. It was a painful experience for his wife and children; and it was an anguishing experience for us, his siblings. As any person who has had experience with cancer knows, sometimes, the complex feelings and lifestyle changes can become as overwhelming for family members and friends. We had all been sailing along so well. Life had been a smooth flow. Then bang. The whole family hit the wall. The shock, the immediate sense of his loss affected everyone in the family. We, his siblings, were so devastated that it blocked our ability to ably assist our sister-in-law and his children to find steps to foster healthy, mutually supportive relationships during that challenging time. We should have provided more help to make it through physically, emotionally, and spiritually.

I personally felt as though a wind was sweeping me away. I was as destabilized as if the ground were rocking under my feet. I could not believe that my brother, my best friend of childhood with whom I had shared the same bed until he was twenty-two and I was nineteen and with whom I had shared so much life together was going to leave us. I should have been stronger and faced the situation with courage, grace, and peace; instead I discovered that I am terribly weak in the face of terrible circumstances.

Cancer has the worst effect on marriages and other long-term partnerships and on the children's vision of life. After a diagnosis of cancer, both spouse and children experience sadness, anxiety, anger, or even hopelessness. In our case in facing the challenges of cancer the siblings remained united and tried to remain close to my brother but probably we could have been more effective by displaying more courage.

Sheila and the children faced this anguishing situation on a daily basis; the siblings tried to help in whatever way possible. At times you truly feel impotent, and you are. Sometimes one becomes overprotective or controlling. You want to know and would like to try to gain some control by becoming an expert in some area of the disease or by keeping the schedule or treatment and communicating with the medical team. Suddenly you learn a vocabulary that is both new and threatening. Adjusting to a shift in roles did not come easily to my brother, who was a physician. As a person who had always been in charge or served as the caregiver, my brother had trouble adjusting to a more dependent role.

Because of his profession, my brother wanted to keep his disease a secret and we did our best to conceal his conditions. When it was too evident from his dramatic weight loss that he was seriously sick, it was painful to lie and to find excuses for his appearance to those friends who asked. At the cemetery on the day of the funeral for Mr. Hennessy, Sheila's father, Sue Hennessy asked me: "Mario, is there anything I can do; I can see that Enrico is not well." Once more, to be loyal to my brother's wish, I lied: "He is OK; it's not a big problem." And I found excuses several times before with other people who had asked. My brother, although very sick, was continuing to see his patients: He needed to keep busy. I imagined that if his patients found out that he was terminally ill, they would have dropped him and he would have felt abandoned. We had little experience with life-threatening illnesses and didn't know what to say or how to act when someone has cancer. It was frightening. We wanted to give emotional and physical support to Sheila and the children, but we were finding out that we needed some of it too.

We were anxious every time Enrico went for a test and tense on finding out the medical updates. Not to exhaust Sheila, we would call Domenico who was following Enrico's condition closely and intensely involved in trying to find a method or a technique that would work. He contacted many cancer centers that were doing experimental trials and he flew to visit a couple of them. His wife could not understand the energy and passion that he was giving to our brother's condition and they fought.

We had all become powerless. We had been able to overcome so many obstacles and had the feeling that we were going to make it. Prayers and hope were keeping us believing that my brother was going to make it. As a family, working together, we had come a long way and we just could not accept that now, in this, we were powerless.

My mother was not around anymore to give us strength with

her faith. I don't know if she would have tried to bring some serenity with her "*è la volontà di Dio*," "It's God's will." My brother, the doctor's, saying would probably have prevailed; "You can give God some problems along the way, but in the end, he always wins."

Reality was constantly forcing us to face the worst. My brother was melting away every day under our very eyes. We were fighting in disbelief. One evening during one of the last chats in his bedroom, while we were alone, he expressed in a resigned tone his concerns for his children. He was especially concerned for his youngest daughter, Erica, and his oldest daughter, Laura. "Probably I was too tough on them. Too severe and demanding. I pushed and pushed them and I gave the impression that I was never happy with their achievements. When I was about to start to letting off the pressure, I was killed." I did not know what to say in that terrible moment, I succeeded in mumbling "Don't worry, everything will be OK." "In a way it is partially my fault for not going to the best surgeon the first time I was operated on. I saved so many lives, and I was not able to make the right decision for myself, and now I have to pay with my life. With three daughters, I cannot even walk down the aisle with any of them. Erica is still too young, still too fragile. I hope she will not be affected too much. Laura is too attached to the skirt of her mother and I don't know if she will get married; I need to make sure that she will have a roof over her head," he said deeply worried. "Worry about yourself now; they will be OK," I said half confused. At which he responded, "What is there to be concerned about myself at this point?" Driving home to Stony Brook that night I cried without restraint.

It was a terrible evening, probably the worst in my life. I made such a stupid remark. Couldn't I have found better words with which to give him some relief? He was looking towards a future from which he had been forcefully cut off. Although he could not be there, he wanted to make sure that his children were not going to have psychological issues and financial problems, that they would complete their educations and have wonderful weddings.

When he passed away, so many people came to pay their respects at the wake and at the funeral, relatives, friends, his hundreds of patients, more and less important people and dignitaries. There was a vast outpouring of love, respect, and solidarity. A lady from the Italian Consulate told me, "He was not just my doctor, he was my father." Even today, eighteen years later, some of his patients still lament his loss.

His loss was very difficult for my father. My brother told us not to tell him how sick he was or of what he suffered. And we honored his request. At the wake, when I accompanied him to the casket he said: "God, why did you punish me like this? I should be there and he should be in my place." It is difficult for any old father to be at the funeral of his son or daughter.

A few days after the funeral, Sheila called the brothers and sisters to tell us that Ambassador Francesco Paolo Fulci had phoned to tell her that he was away in South America when my brother passed away and wanted to pay a visit to the family. While he was in New York as Italian Ambassador to the United Nations he had become one of my brother's patients and, as in many cases, a friend. He came to my brother's house with his wife, expressed his condolences and friendship to the family, and asked if we could accompany him to the cemetery to place some flowers on the tomb.

When my father passed away three years later, he had lived a full life. He was ninety-three years old and until three months before he died he had lived in the comfort of his house completely physically fit. At the end he had become very proud of his children. "Because of God's will," as he used to say, he had had much satisfaction, at the end with a bitter-sweet undertone. The last time he was a patient at Mt. Vernon Hospital, he said, "Who would have thought in this hospital, where I worked as a gardener when I came to America, my son become Chairman of the Board. God gives and takes away."

When he was released from the hospital, with a heart that was giving out, I took him to my house to give him the support he needed. But after a few days he had to be taken to the emergency room of our hospital. Because the treatment did not seem adequate to my brothers, in two days I had to take him by ambulance to a Westchester hospital where two of my brothers were on staff.

When he was released, my brother Biagio with the support of his wife Kathy, a trained nurse, brought him to their home where after about a month he died surrounded by his family.

Our life had been like the life of millions of other families, like a rose garden: full of dreams, satisfaction, joys, trepidations, anxieties, sacrifices, obstacles, and sorrows. The passing away of my brother was a kind of watershed because it broke the collective aspirations of a family unit. Yes, life continued, and had to continue. But deep down, consciously and unconsciously we could feel that it was not the same. Yet we all managed to go on. Miraculously, my brother's children and his wife continued on his well-established trajectory and honored their father. Under the strong direction of Sheila, the children reached what my brother was dreaming they would achieve. How I wished so many times to speak to him to hear how he was savoring their success!

FOURTEEN

In 1978 I decided to take a trip back home to show my children where my family came from and where I spent the first twenty years of my life. I prepared the trip with a lot of excitement and expectations: I was returning as a well-established university professor accompanied by my wife Lois and my three daughters, Pamela, Cristina, and Elizabeth. I had planned to visit some culturally relevant sites that would satisfy some of their curiosity from their school lessons and readings and would enrich their young cultural formation. But, most of all, I was eager to take them where I had spent my childhood and to show them what propelled my family and me to leave for America. I believed that it was a natural desire of emigrants and, I assumed, a natural desire of their children and, thus, also of my children.

The tourist part of the trip went well. They certainly were fascinated by the Coliseum, St. Peter's, the Pantheon, and the archeological sites of Pompeii. Who would not be at their very young ages? After they tasted their first gelato and Nutella, they became hooked on things that helped make the trip more enjoyable. Encounters with my relatives also went well, even though it was tiring for me to interpret all the time because of the language barrier. My wife and I did a terrible job teaching Italian to our children; we waited until they went to high school and college to learn how to communicate in Italian. Big failure on our part!

Although I very much wanted my children to get to know the family, I was more anxious that they should connect with my past, the farm where I grew up with my siblings, the places that were intimately tied with our lives, the schools were we learned that there was a world beyond our farm. We went to the Gran Potenza to see the farmhouse and its surroundings. While driving there, memories flowed back without the need to dig or seek them out.

We don't remember days, we remember moments. Digging in our memory is like reading. When we read, we are not looking for new ideas, but to see our own thoughts given the seal of confirmation on a printed page. The words that strike us are those that awaken an echo in a zone we have already made our own—the place where we live—and the vibration enables us to find fresh starting points within ourselves. For some reason the image of the nights we spent on the *aia infilando il tabacco* popped up in my memory. The women that came to work for us, sitting in a circle on the stones telling stories and guessing at riddles, greatly amused us children, who stood around rubbing our sleepy eyes. All around us, hills with hamlets in the distance that resembled clusters of fireflies stimulated our imagination and, somehow, again tickled mine.

Our farm was on top of a hill, the Gran Potenza, about two miles from the boundary of the city of Benevento. It was typical of the area: It did not have running water, electricity, or any other amenities that people living in the city take for granted. We were so close to the city and still so far away considering the way we lived. We were close enough to go to the city schools and every day we went to the city, walked its paved streets, met its people, saw how they lived in their apartments, spoke to our classmates the city kids—but we didn't have anything in common with that life. We lived on the land with the animals and had a completely different life.

Living on the Gran Potenza offered the advantage of having a spectacular view of the world; the hill offered a three hundred sixty degree view of the landscape. On the east side we had a full view of the city of Benevento, on the southwest there was a chain of hills, followed by another chain of higher hills, and then, high in the background, the mountains. In the North there were also hills, but with smoother elevations that provided a sense of depth to the landscape. At night all those hills offered an magical spectacle with the blinking lights of the villages scattered all around. But as I grew up, life became increasingly harsh on those hills. There was no charm, especially in the bleak days of winter, both for the children and their parents who had to make a living from the land.

In living on a farm, children make a gradual progression from jobs such as helping with the minor, light tasks of feeding the animals to harder chores like milking cows, and completely assuming harder and heavier tasks when they are older. We also endured that process. In retrospect, I tend to believe that we learned how to give and take from farming and from being involved in farming; we learned that when something needed to be done to do it as best we could. We instinctively learned to take responsibility. Growing up on a farm allows children to understand plant, human, and animal relationships and gain skills and experiences that will help them even if they do not choose to become farmers. Working in the hot sun or cold rain for 60 hours a week I have come to believe that there isn't much a farmer can't do in life if he put his mind to it.

We all have challenging days at the office or at home. Some days are just "off" and we're not at the top of our game. But cattle, crops, and weather don't care if you're having a hard time. The cattle need to eat, and the hay must be baled. Often the bootstraps just have to be pulled up, and you must plow through even if you don't feel like it. Ex-farm kids don't have a well-known work ethic for nothing!

Farm kids have grown up hearing "Early to bed and early to rise, makes a person healthy, wealthy, and wise." My father always said, you can stay up as late as you want, just plan on getting up at daybreak to start work on any number of jobs he had planned for the day. My older brother Enrico was always the one with the alarm on: He had the task of milking the cow at four in the morning.

Work on the farm has been hard always and everywhere. And it doesn't really seem fair when we see stories on the news of Mother Nature doling out her share of "uncertainties" and cataclysms to our farmers. Years ago there were no governmental safety nets or measures that provided a financial cushion for farmers who constantly faced unpredictable weather or subsidies for rural communities and environmentally sensitive land. Even if the farmers were expecting a good crop, that didn't mean everything was going to go their way. Not even close. On the Gran Potenza we were sure of one thing: lack of rain during the summer. Flooding, drought, disease, and other uncertainties of life always hovered close to our farm. The connection to the land, albeit special, is also stressful.

Life on a farm is different for kids. How many times going home from school I would think "Some of the other kids in school don't have to do all this farm work!" When they went home they played with their friends or watched after-school specials on TV instead of heading out to do chores. Looking back, I must admit that we were molded with a stronger fiber by farm life and we learned lessons from it that city kids could not experience. "There are always going to be others that don't seem to be working as hard as you are," and my father would say that "on the freeway of life there will always be cars in front of you and cars behind you."

Life on a farm created in us a predisposition to endurance and family unity. A farm does not allow for vacation time — at least not in the way that urban and suburban families take vacations. A vacation for my father was on Sunday when he did not work in the fields and had to tend to the small daily routine tasks. My family, as most other families I knew, always sat down for meals together, including breakfast. We were expected to be on time, help serve, clear, and clean up the table. We were also expected to participate in conversation. We all ate the same food, no special menus or diets were considered.

We ate outside, in front of our farmhouse under a huge birch tree from spring until the middle of fall. Those early experiences with food have imprinted habits and tastes that have extended into adulthood. We carried to America a love for gardening, cooking, and sharing meals with family and friends and have continued those habits as adults with our own families as my wife and I have done.

I didn't realize it at the time, but those days growing up on the farm would shape my siblings and me into who we are today. It would also instill in us lessons that we have used for the rest of our lives. Those lessons learned on the farm are used by some of our children in their professional lives, their cooking business and wealth management business. If I were to write a "Growing Up on the Farm Lessons of Life" book, I might include this gem: "You must make hay while the sun shines."

It's obvious that in the days of old, farming life was tough. It is still a tough occupation. Nevertheless, I look back fondly on my younger years growing up on the farm. The teamwork among my brothers, sisters, and me in accomplishing chores and projects helped cement our close relationship today. Little did I know at the time, that I was probably attending the best school available on work ethics.

And here I was returning to the house of my childhood anxious to have my children taste the life I had lived at their age. In no terms could they have felt on their skin the sensations I experienced walking along those country paths or open fields of my childhood, nor could they have smelled what mother nature had given us throughout the seasons or during the various hours of days and nights. But my words, in my encounter with my past, might have conveyed something new and real, something potent, that could have touched them intimately. I had come from the land, and I carried with me to America, beneath my skin, in my breath, and in my consciousness, a bundle of feelings, perceptions that by osmosis they were carrying unconsciously.

But our encounter with my past could not have been more dismal. The house, empty for many years, showed no life. Dust blew in the hot summer sun. Silence! No children, no running, yelling, escaping. Our dog, that had welcomed me back in my first brief trip two years after I had emigrated, had long gone. Seeing him was the most emotional moment of my return. Although two years had gone by, he recognized me immediately and jumped all over me, licking my feet, running around me in circles and then returning, barking in a lament; I understood exactly what he was saying in his language and he almost moved me to tears. He recognized my voice, my smell, my look and was reconnecting with our lost affection for each other. He remained attached to my feet, almost in fear of being separated again, for the rest of the day that I was there. He went on the long walk through our land with me and when he felt more secure that I wasn't going to disappear again, he walked before me to trace the old paths that were almost lost in the overgrown grass. At a certain point he ran ahead a couple of hundred feet; his memory was still intact—he was checking the path for snakes, my worst fear of living on the farm. I called him with my old whistle, and he ran back, again jumping around my legs and licking my shoes. I cherished those moments of reconnection with the past which made me forget all the tribulations and hardships of living on the farm; Rodomonte did not know that it was a fleeting moment; my re-found loyal friend was not aware of that and I was doing everything possible to heighten the joy of that reconnection.

The memory of that encounter heightened the sense of desolation on this trip in which I intended to teach my kids about my past. Gradually I became aware that it was going to be a painful experience. My children were too young to understand what I wanted to reveal to them. I had dreamed for a long time about this trip to connect my children with my childhood, which was very different from theirs. The heat of the day, the field flies, the rocky or brushy paths we were walking on, were too annoying to get their attention. I was not angry for the lack of interest. They were too young to understand what I was trying to do, and growing up in the upper middle class of Long Island made it even more difficult. Refraining from showing my disappointment, I made some general comments about the trees that had been cut on the property and how neatly cultivated the land used to be, and then I took them to the car and we went back to San Leucio, the village house where we were staying.

My wife prepared the lunch. After eating we went for a gelato, and then we went to take the customary afternoon nap. But it was not easy for me to close my eyes, never mind fall asleep. I leaned over to my wife and told her that I had to go to the city to buy some food and then pass by the Gran Potenza because I had forgotten the carton of cigarettes I planned to give to my friend Albino. Going back to the Gran Potenza I took the road that I had taken on foot probably more than a couple hundred times, usually with our donkey to bring a load of different kinds of foods from our property in San Leucio. I knew that road intimately because the trips were not taken with pleasure. With my brother Enrico I had learned how to handle a loaded donkey. We did not have to worry about cars because in those years very few people had a car, but also because it was a dirt road, and therefore not suitable for cars. However, occasionally we had to deal with ferocious dogs from other farmhouses that would come to the road and bark at us fiercely. And sometimes we would find a bunch of kids there who, to break their monotony, would try to start fights with us.

This time I was on that same road in a car; the road had been paved and there was light car traffic. I drove at a slow pace because I wanted to see how the landscape had changed and I wanted to refresh my memory about different spots. I passed in front of the cemetery, a landmark for me because I always saw it with a sense of sorrow for the scenes of pain and crying it evoked, especially on All Souls Day when people went to pay respect to their lost ones. The high walls surrounding the cemetery, the tall cypress trees and the memories of candles, flowers, and crying people always created in me a sense of fear and anxiety. If I passed in front of the cemetery in the dark, either very early in the morning or in the late evening, I would attach myself to the load on the donkey and walk with my eyes closed afraid that a ghost from a fresh grave would appear! These were fears that many of us had because of the way we grew up facing death. This time, passing in front of it in a car in daylight I did not have any concerns; life had already taught me that dead people cannot harm anybody and that living people, instead, should be feared for the harm they can provoke.

Driving the seven-mile trip, memories of incidents popped up. At a halfway point along the way, as the road started to go down the hill on the Madonna della Salute, the spot where the fog in the early morning was very thick, I remembered the intense cold I felt one winter morning. The cold had gone into my nails and I was feeling excruciating pain and started to cry. Enrico told me to keep my hands in my pockets so that they would warm up with my body heat, but I was not feeling any relief. The cold was so sharp under my nails that it was unbearable. The survival instinct made my brother give a suggestion *in extremis*: "Piss on your fingers slowly and rub them gently." I did not hesitate a second to execute his suggestion. The pain gradually subsided and we both rejoiced in the novel solution. Even though I never had a pair of gloves, I never again had to use that extreme solution; the pockets of my pants gave me the protection I needed.

Driving another couple of miles I reached the spot where we had a terrible encounter with a group of kids from the area. I don't know why, but they started to throw stones at us. They knew that we were not from their area; the donkey loaded with firewood gave a clear indication that we were just passing by. My brother instructed me to take care of the donkey and push it to walk faster while he stayed in back and provided the cover by responding with his own stone throwing, collecting them from the street. No one was wounded in the battle, but the incident created apprehension every time we passed that spot.

When I arrived at the Gran Potenza it was late afternoon and life was returning to the fields after the siesta. I don't know why but I wanted to calmly see the farmhouse and the land that held so much of my early experience of life. There was nothing in particular that I wanted to check, but I had a burning desire to see again the places where my family and I had lived and struggled and that I had left without much pain or remorse. I had traveled the world, I had read a lot, I had become a university professor; what could I find back in that house, in that piece of land besides to say, "Here is what I was when I was born"? Probably we need a village, a place, if nothing else, for the pleasure of saying, "Here are the seeds of my life." Your village means that you're not alone, that you know there's something of you in the people, in the plants, stones and soil, so that even when you are not there, there is something that waits to welcome you. There may be a subconscious desire that makes us look for that somewhere that makes you say, "Here is what I was, and this is what I am"; a somewhere that makes you believe that it belongs to you, that somewhere in which you try to grasp the essence of your origin and, therefore, of your identity. I had been around the world enough to know that all human flesh is basically the same and that anyone is worth as much as another, and it's probably because of this that one gets tired and tries to find his roots so that his flesh is worth a little more and lasts a little longer than a round of seasons. Even the dog, when I returned the first time, instinctively celebrated our reunion, probably to recapture his lost past. He smelled my legs and jumped in ecstasy.

From the front of the house, on top of a hill shaped like a cone with its slopes going down the valleys—on one side to the city, the others to the Serretella River, to the Sabato River, and the Calore River—I saw the landscape with which I grew up and which I had carried in my memory in America and kept frozen in time. The hills and the mountains around, the pathways, the clusters of trees, the farmsteads scattered as I had seen them day after day, year after year. Leaning against a twisted fig tree, I thought about the hot summers when we had to help my parents in the fields, especially to thresh wheat, with sickle in our hands bent for eight or nine hours under the scorching sun and a temperature in the upper nineties.

The sun was shining on the hills to the east; it was made stronger by its reflection from the dry soil that I'd forgotten. At that time of day, instead coming from the sky, the heat was rising from below, from the ground, from the cracked ground where every trace of green seemed to have been eaten up and turned to dry twigs. In a way I liked that heat, I liked its smell; there was something of me in that smell. It reminded me of hay making and tobacco curing, of the many tastes and desires I still had. I kept an eye on the fields; I almost wished that my life was still ahead, and that I could change it. I looked again at those hills, those paths, and the dog from our next-door neighbor lying down gasping for air in the strong heat. I thought that if I hadn't escaped eighteen years before, that would have been my fate. I grieved at the thought.

While absorbed in those visual thoughts, Albino, our friend from next door, called me. I was happily surprised to see him. I knew that many of our friends had left for the north and did not know who had stayed behind. He became my informant and my interlocutor. I learned that two of his older siblings had migrated to Milano, as did so many other young people from our area. It would have been my destiny, too, had I not had the door to America opened for me. Albino remained to continue life in the old mold. I did not ask why he did not join them, but migration is not for everybody, and poverty and hardship alone are not strong enough forces to move people out.

While we were chatting, Albino's wife passed by, barefoot and sunbaked and watched me with suspicion. She was a strong woman who had worked in the fields like all the other women and endured harsh conditions, carrying water, heavy baskets, and bundles of firewood, going barefoot in the rain, eating beans and lentils. I felt almost embarrassed by my clothes, my shirt, my shoes. How long had it been since I'd gone barefoot? Turning to the woman I asked, "Are the wells still there?" She nodded yes and came closer probably to walk me to see them. I said not to trouble herself because I knew the whole place foot by foot and I could go around and see everything at my pace on my own.

Albino and I sat under a tree in front of his house and chatted for a few hours about the people who had passed away, those who had emigrated and the changes that had taken place on our hills. "Why did they cut down the birch in front of the house?" I asked with dismay, "it was such an intimate part of our lives." "Your uncle," he replied, "eliminated it because it was too big and the branches were rubbing against the house and the roof." The birch was a point of reference for all of us. Under the large crown of foliage there was a round marble table around which we spent collectively as a family and individually our best and the most enjoyable times. Especially in the hot summer days when the heat was unbearable inside, life moved under that birch tree; breakfast, dinner, supper, breaks, and recreation were spent there in the open breeze. The birch was our gym, dining room, recreational room, and when it was extremely hot, it was also a bedroom for us boys, and our refuge, our dream house. My brothers and I had a passion for climbing it, and I don't know why. Probably the breeze was cooler up there. Probably it was an exercise to escape boredom. Probably I enjoyed the climb because it provided me with a sense of escape to dream. From up there, I had a bigger view of my world and I had a sense of domain and control. Before coming to America I had not traveled anywhere, but I had dreamed a lot. I knew that the world did not end where the sun set behind the Taburno Mountain and I wanted to see what could be seen high up from the ground. A couple of times, sitting on one of the highest branches and leaning against the trunk of the birch, I fell asleep and put my life in danger.

Cutting down that tree had also destroyed a wonderful record of special events in our lives. On the bark of the central trunk we had carved the dates of what was memorable for each of us; Enrico had put down the date when he finished high school; I wanted to remember the first time I kissed a girl; Uncle Vincent wrote the date of his first visit to Italy after he had been released from the Korean War. Most of those dates meant something only to those who had recorded them in the soft bark. Some of us had recorded more than one date. Carving was easy in the soft bark with a knife. The incisions took some time to show because they had to mature in the bark. They attracted the attention of those who came to visit us and sometime they became a guessing game. Even the boys living in the farmhouse next to us made a couple of incisions. I reminded Albino of them and he said that he had recorded the date when his grandmother had passed away. "He didn't have to cut down the entire tree. If he would have cut just the branches touching the house, he could have spared the tree and preserved so many of our memories," said Albino harshly.

Albino talked to me in a subdued tone now and related to me how things had changed on those hills. Many people had died, the children had grown up, and many had left. He told me who was living in the old houses; and some were the same people we knew — Pepe, Ciullo, Cantuscio, Viola, Salomone. I told him that I remembered their goats and sheep grazing in the fields. I especially remembered their dogs. When a dog barked at night I knew exactly whose dog it was. Every sound and every smell traveling on those hills was unique. "Do you remember the cherry tree that Gramazio had on top of the hill? That bastard cut it down." I knew the story. For a couple of years in a row, while Gramazio was taking a nap in the afternoon, Albino and my brother Nino climbed the tree and stole the cherries. Not able to contain his rage, Gramazio cut down the tree. He had tried to keep the boys off the tree by tying under the crown a circle of thorny branches, but the boys had succeeded in climbing it just the same.

Gradually I realized that time had washed away many things that were there, important landmarks of my childhood world. Looking up the hill I noticed that several trees had been cut down. "Mario," Albino said, "the land now is plowed with tractors, and fields are worked with machines and trees are big obstacles." We started to walk in the semi abandoned fields and talked about the way we had worked the land in our childhood. I could not believe we had run around and played so much between the house and the top of the hill. My siblings and I knew every square meter of that land, we had stepped on every centimeter, especially the areas where the tobacco was cultivated and needed our constant attention. We passed by the Vallo where fresh grass abounded more than other places, and I remembered the freak accident that almost cost my sister Matilde's hand when she went to gather grass for the cow and fell on a sickle. She needed five stiches at the emergency room, but no official complained that children shouldn't be subjected to dangerous work. Nothing was there anymore; only memories.

We walked toward the *cava*, the side of the property that touched the public road, a wide dirt road. The oak trees, too, had been cut down, but the memory of girls sunbathing was still alive. For a few summers a couple of sisters came from the city to tan at the edge of our property. I remember the girls, especially the blonde one who was so blonde that her head blended with the *spighe di grano*. I was happy to have such special guests on our property because of the dreams that they kindled. One day I wanted to appreciate their beauty more and decided to have a closer look. When I saw them coming up from down the hill, I went to a spot close to the place where they bathed and I hid in a bush. When they arrived, they put down the bags, spread the blankets, and started to change. They lifted up their skirts and put on the lower part of their bikinis. Then they proceeded to take off their blouses to put on the top part of the bikini. Every movement was so innocent and natural. It was like a dream. And what about my spying? I had never been at a beach; the only times we would see women's legs above their knees was in our dreams and when we went to the circus. We grew up accustomed to see women nursing babies exposing their breasts; it was so natural and so functional that we boys never attached any sexual meaning to it. Seeing a couple of girl in bikinis lying in the sun in an open field stimulated a fantasy that coursed from ecstasy to a maniacal stupor. At age sixteen, I was trying to make some sense of that scene in the soft breeze that filtered through the dry grass and the bush were I was hiding. I had been in America and I had lived through the sex revolution of the sixties and seventies and now that moment of my past left me perplexed. When I grew up sex was more consumed in our dreams, in our imagination. It was made of smiles and furtive looks. Sometimes it found expression on the walls of the bathrooms in our schools or on our school desks. Oh God, how many desires and compliments for the physically well-endowed girls; sometimes, even female teachers got attention. Sometimes the compliments were expressed in verses with a kissing rhyme! I wondered what happened to those dreams of trying to approach a girl to steal a smile or to have a kiss? I wondered if it was better to struggle to have something highly desired or to have it within reach at will. Yes, too many desires and fantasies were burned, but in that world of hardships, all those illusions made our lives full of dreams.

"Mario, do you remember the *cisterna* at Fantozzi? The water that we used to steal at night? That too is gone." The *cisterna* had vanished several years before we left for America. It was a reservoir for the brick factory down the valley. Water was the big thorn in our life living on that hill. Nobody had it. My father dug four deep wells, but no miracle wanted to bless us. He built two of them so that during the rainy winter they would fill up and provide us with water for about seven months of the year, but for the other five months we had to look for it wherever we could find it, and sometimes we had to steal it. For many years the source was a cistern belonging to the factory of fire-bricks at the foot of the hill. The cistern was close to our property up the hill where we went at night because the factory officials had told us that the cistern was private property and we could not trespass. I don't think that they wanted to deny us the water because of the cost; most likely it was for safety. We had made holes in the perimeter wall to climb to the top, and stood on the wall to get the water bucket by bucket. There was a danger that we might slip and end up in the water. When the cistern was demolished, we had to find another source. For a couple of years I went early in the morning to steal the water from a well down the hill. My father would get the donkey ready with two barrels and I would do the rest. I had to get the water from the well and pour it into the barrels on the donkey; but they were too high for me and I could not reach them to pour the water. I solved the problem by pulling the buckets of water from the well while standing on the well. One morning the lady of the house caught me stealing the water and was enraged by the way I was doing it. If the donkey had moved slightly I could have ended up in the well. She went to my house and told my father that she did not want to see me near her property again. We had to find another source. We came up with the idea of the running fountain at Rione Libertà. It was further and had to be done very early in the morning because the police did not permit us to get water at a city fountain with a donkey. So for the rest of the time that we lived on the Gran Potenza, for about three months a year, my father would wake me up around four in the morning and I would fulfill what became my task. My brother Enrico graduated from it as soon as I became eligible for the job. He had to milk the cow and Nino had been promoted to bringing the milk down to the main road where the milkman passed by to collect it.

Having a donkey, Albino reminded me, we were better off than they were because his sisters had to carry the *lancelle* of water on their heads. We got closer to the house; the cowshed was lifeless without the smell of fresh manure. No part of the roof had collapsed, but everything conveyed a sense of abandonment. Nothing was there anymore. Nothing was the same. Step after step I was struck with a feeling of absence. What was no longer had become something else. I don't doubt that even if someone had kept the cow, the sheep, the pig and the other animals we had, that I would not have been able to sense the old environment with the sensitivity of my childhood; I was now an adult who had lived in the city, worked in factories, and was enjoying the comfort of office work. In the process we acquire but also we lose. What was no longer is and what is left only exists in memory. It's probably part of our destiny. I understood what it meant existentially to have emigrated. Again I was asking myself if it had been worth it to come back to visit the place of my childhood and youth. A man is never completely alone in this world because, at worst, he has the company of his childhood, youth, and by the time he grows up, what he used to be. Memory can be our curse but also our constant nourishment.

It was almost sunset; and the sun was about to slide down behind the Taburno. The red sky was as it had always been; nature was repeating itself, as did the seasons of the year. Looking down the Sabato River, I saw the train coming from Avellino. No smoke came off the locomotive. I was waiting for the whistle that used to travel for miles to reach us on top of the hill in the morning, serving as a clock to inform us that it was time to wash up on the loggia and get ready to go to school. Sometimes on lazy summer afternoons the train made me wonder about the stations and the villages it crossed and where all those people on it were going. Now that I have seen a lot of the world and I know that it is made of many interconnected villages and cities, I don't know whether as a boy I was that wrong at all. A village means not being alone, knowing that in the people who live there, in the trees, in the ground there is something that is yours that even when you are not there, remains waiting for you. We all need a village, a place where we can anchor and probably that's why I was there again. But it's not easy to be there untroubled. One understands these things with time and experience. Probably deep down there was the belief that the past holds a secret that will unlock the mystery of personal identity. My memory almost acted as if I were trying to put together the pieces of a puzzle.

There is something that I cannot understand. For someone who left, being neither fish nor fowl, I should have been pleased; and indeed I am. But is it enough? I liked the Bronx and we loved Stony Brook; but I would like to know why my Stony Brook is what it is in a world that spins around.

Standing on the *aia* in front of the house, Albino reminded me of the times we played ball and ended up fighting. I played a lot with my brother Enrico. We took turns in kicking ten penalty kicks while one of us was the goalie under the loggia. It was the only game we could play, but cheating or the suspicion of cheating very often broke the game up on a sour note. I loved soccer and would have loved to go to the stadium to see the games on Sunday. At game time I would hang around on the *aia* in front of our house to see if I could get a sense of how it was going. The stadium was in the valley and the noise of the spectators with all its passion reached us. Particularly when the wind was favorable, I could follow the game merely by hearing the noise, the whistles, the boos, and screams. When our team scored I jumped as though I were present in the stadium. When the whistles deafened your ears, I could imagine and sometime even hear the screams at the referee: "*arbitro venduto*," "*arbitro cornuto*." I certainly would have loved to be there to add my own insults! I asked Albino, "Do you go to see some of the games?" "I don't have the desire anymore; if you don't feel a passion for it, it's irrelevant," he said calmly.

When Albino left, I had the feeling that he had lost the passion because he had remained trapped in the life to which he had resigned himself. He was the lazy one of his family and never sought challenges. I don't know if digging in our memories had the same vibrations.

Before going back to my wife and children, I wanted to see how the house looked inside. I went upstairs where the two bedrooms were; two bedrooms for a family of ten. When I entered I found most of the furniture intact. There it was, in the left corner, the bed where I slept with my brother Enrico. It was a single bed but we managed to make it for two by placing a board between the wall and the bed. It was OK in wintertime when our bodies helped each other to keep warm.

The dining table was covered with dust and abandoned old bleached newspapers. I could see my mother filling the dishes of pasta or beans and potatoes and the perennial salad with vinegar and oil; I could hear the ringing voices of my siblings and the noise of forks and spoons in dishes; I could smell the garlic and tomato sauce. And I could hear the many laughs, screams, and some moral lessons delivered from my mother or my father.

The brazier was there still in one corner of the room. In winter it was our savior and our unifying force. My mother would sit to knit or mend clothes and we would study in a circle. When my mother noticed that we were not focused on our studies anymore, she would start the Rosary. We had to pray for many things: for clement weather, for good health (especially for my father's, the breadwinner of the family) and for protecting our family. Our faith nourished our strength when we faced the harsh life on the farm and it sustained us when we emigrated. With religion came also moral lessons: "If you wish to travel far and fast, travel light," she used to say. "Shake off all your envies, jealousies, unforgiveness, selfishness, and fears and, to be even a better *cristiano*, give a ready hand rather than a ready tongue." No question, lessons are not given, they are taken, and for the most part we took them.

I was dismayed looking around. I felt like Totò in *Cinema Paradiso* when he went back, after so many years, to visit the movie house where he worked as a boy. I was seeing only ghosts. There were no connecting threads anymore. It was a *Paradiso* lost forever. Nothing could be recovered to forge continuity.

Before leaving, I saw a bale of hay downstairs in front of the *capannone*. It was an old bale and did not have the smell of fresh hay we used to have around to feed the animals. It had been a long day, and I decided to sit on it to rest for a few minutes. It had gotten dark. I remembered right after the war when, as children, my brother and I would sit on a bale of hay and watch imaginary movies on the wall of the house. Down the valley from the Appian Way, the occasional cars that would pass, usually with their high beams on, would provide us with entertainment; the lights in motion going through a tree would project images in motion on the wall. My brother and I would give form to those images and invent a story. Inevitably one of us would make fun of the imagination of the other and this would put an end to the free movie *all'aperto*. It was a nice way to kill a summer evening, when it worked.

I lay down on the bale and closed my eyes thinking back to those times. No television, no radio, no toys, and no kids to play with. We were left only with our inventiveness, and we never suffered for not having much; the other people on those hills were in the same boat, and many were in worse condition. I don't know if children in the city that had more than we did experienced more satisfactions or pleasures. I fell asleep. I must have slept for no more than ten minutes. I woke up because I dreamed that I was cutting the grass for the cow and a snake jumped at me. The fear of finding a snake in the fields always haunted me. That fear remained in my consciousness and, although latent, created an adverse feeling for reptiles even in America and made me dislike people who had snakes as pets.

Before getting in the car to return to my wife and children, I remembered that I had a carton of cigarettes for Peppe Salomone, the person who helped us go to school with clean shoes. It was too late to go down the hill to say hello. I called Albino and asked him to make the delivery. "Mario, he died last year, and that house is now closed, abandoned," Albino told me with reluctance. It was sad news because I had always kept in mind that when I went back to the Gran Potenza I had to express our gratitude for what he and his wife did for us. To go to school we used a path through the fields of two houses. After Viola, we reached the Salomones. Their house had a long paved driveway that led to the road to the city. We used their house to change from our farmer shoes full of mud to clean shoes. They would leave the door of a storage room unlocked on the first floor of their house for our use. We would go inside, change shoes, and go to school in a "civilized" manner. That was our room; not only would we leave our shoes there and an old umbrella in case we were caught in the rain, but we would also use it as shelter during inclement weather. I remembered the day I was going back home from school and I was caught in a snow storm, without gloves or a hat and in shorts — in those years most boys wore shorts even in winter because they cost less. Peppe Salomone saw me as I was approaching their house and called me to come into their kitchen. "Come here, come inside and warm up next to the fireplace before you go home." Inside I found my brother Enrico who had pulled in a few minutes earlier for the same reason.

The Salomones were one of the few blessings we had living on the Gran Potenza. We did not like to say that we lived on a farm because of the stigma it carried. The shoes we wore were one of the indicators of where we came from when we were at school. In those years farmers were still placed on the lowest step of the social ladder. When I came to America, notwithstanding the discrimination that was still palpable, though veiled, being Italian American was a tremendous emancipation from being an Italian farmer.

Driving back to San Leucio that evening I carried bittersweet feelings. I found in my memory moments of my past, some more vivid than others, and I was neither happy nor sad because these were a mix of alternating sensations. Some were very gratifying and I felt blessed for having experienced those moments in my life, but there was also a sense of loss, not just for the people that had left or died, but because life doesn't allow pleasant moments to return.

The trip back to my childhood with my wife and my children was not what I expected. I wonder if I had taken that trip through an album of photographs what I would have found and felt. Certainly it would not have been the same journey, and there is no way to compare them. We did not own a camera and so we don't have a collection of photographs that captured moments of that part of our lives, but I am sure that it would not have been remotely close to what memory could disclose. I was at peace with myself. The encounters with my memory did not unearth anything traumatic; memories of concentration camps or internments, sexual abuse or molestation. It was not a journey of survival and courage. No one of us, thank God, carry big scars from big wounds, which tell a story, a story that says, "I have survived." Put in the context of human experience, it has the appearance of a dull journey. We did not even have to deal with divorce of our parents or other family misfortunes. Even though it was an unsettling voyage because no one can rediscover anew the enchantments of childhood, I was happy that nothing had been stashed away somewhere in my memory to produce a traumatic imprint in our lives.

FIFTEEN

The journey back to my childhood with my wife and my children confirmed the old saying: "one does not step in the same river twice." The next day I took my children to Benevento, the city where we went to school and church, shopped, and lived that little bit of "civil" life we could afford. We visited some of the churches, the squares, the beautiful city park, and we passed in front of the schools that my siblings and I attended. The elementary school was the closest to our house, but the middle and high schools were quite a distance away, about four miles. The painful walk was in winter, not so much for the distance, but for the inclement weather. Benevento is in a valley and almost every morning in winter is engulfed in a thick fog; between the rain, snow, cold, and fog, going to school in winter was arduous.

We enjoyed a leisurely stroll in the city. The girls had a gelato and learned some historic facts about the Sannites and the Roman roots of the city. I remembered the places where I walked, between the ages of thirteen to sixteen, with my brother Enrico and a couple of his friends. When I got older, I took those walks with my friend Franco Baccari. There was not much to do in the city besides going to the movies and ambling along the main street or hanging around a piazza. To go to the movies we needed money, which could we could manage two or three times a year. Strolling did not cost anything; it was a good way to kill time and to see people and, hopefully, be seen. Our aim was to see girls, especially those few for whom we felt a special attraction. On Saturday evening Franco and I would buy three cigarettes—we preferred Jubeck because they were light—and would keep them for the right moment. When we saw girls who were out for the same reason, we would light up a cigarette and smoke with the air of popular movie stars. That was the ritual to convey the message that we were strutting, looking for some attention. It was a ritual that the girls knew very well, and they responded or not responded according to their liking or disliking of us. They knew all our movements and could practically read our minds.

We had *crushes*. All kids have crushes when they are teenagers. Aren't we made to fall in love? And aren't we made to love? Given the culture of the times, we had to create situations to see, meet, to steal a smile or a *"ciao"* from a girl that we liked or were infatuated with. We would risk sending a written note in class or a message by a friend. I still remember the note that I wrote to a girl about whom I was crazily infatuated. To win her heart I wrote: *"Noi siamo un'anima sola con un solo destino ... e come gli astri del cielo staremo per sempre insieme."* It sounds so banal today with Facebook and Twitter, but when I wrote it I truly felt what I was saying. Sometimes we would hope that a girl would drop something — probably intentionally — and we would race to be the first to retrieve it so as to have an occasion to introduce ourselves. But, then, because of fear or nerves, we were not able to find a way to relate. We would be like jerks. Do you remember how Totò behaved in *Cinema Paradiso* when the girl he admired dropped her pen box and he ran to get it to bring it to her? It happened to us boys a few times. Occasions had to be invented for that hoped-for encounter. The result could have been an innocent handshake, and that was enough to make us happy. Those were the years of first loves and heartbreaks; the years when you learn that love doesn't always have a fable's ending.

Many girls in those days walked arm in arm and boys did the same. There was no other message in that way of strolling. In fact, many girls walked arm in arm with their mothers. For a boy to walk alone with a girl meant that you had made the giant step of being engaged to get married. Girls were part of our fantasies. And the fantasies could be realized only to the extent of receiving a fleeting smile or a soft *ciao*.

To go a step further with our dreams we had to use other strategies. To see the legs of girls above their knees we had to take advantage of Mother Nature's help. On a windy day, the best spot was on the bridge over the river. The wind would often lift their dresses and we would have our thrills. Sometimes we would walk back and forth on that bridge hoping that Mother Nature would offer again that special excitement.

Balconies also offered some rare opportunities. In those days girls wore skirts and dresses more than pants, and miniskirts had not yet arrived. Whenever we saw girls standing on a balcony we would change our course if need be to pass under the balcony and look up at the right moment. The girls were astute and often teased us. If they understood our intentions, they would step inside and wait until we passed. One time, three girls had a lot of fun with us. The third time we passed under the balcony, they had a bucket of water ready. When we passed, one of them dumped it on us and said, "I hope we cooled you off!" We liked to brag about the "*panorama*" we had seen, but that time it was the girls' turn to brag, I imagine, about how they cooled off a couple of hot guys.

While walking on the *Corso* I unexpectedly met one of my classmates Antonio DeNigris, "What a surprise to see *l'Americano* here," he said. We embraced and chatted for a while. Since the kids were becoming impatient, we stopped at a bar for a gelato. We tried to catch up mostly on our personal life, above all about our work. Not to bore the children to death, we cut it short. We exchanged addresses and phone numbers and parted.

Other acquaintances greeted me as *l'Americano*. That's the way my siblings and other Italian emigrants were very often greeted when they went back to "the old country." It was a strange situation. At work and in social settings, I was still perceived as Italian, but for the Italians I had become an American. Legally I was an American with American citizenship at which point I automatically lost my Italian citizenship. Italy did not allow dual citizenship. Certainly the melting pot of the sixties had not melted our heritage. Our *Italianità* had not been absorbed by conformity. We had remained largely unassimilated and preserved to a great extent our distinctiveness.

I had worked in an American factory, I had gone through studies in American universities, I was teaching in an American university; in a way I had become part of mainstream America without putting aside my ethnicity — in the privacy of our homes we were still practicing our customs while in public life we were embracing American civic life. Publicly I was perceived as an Italian, but when I went to Italy I was the *Americano*.

I, like most immigrants, grappled with a dual identity. However, I never really faced the question, "How am I balancing the dual identity?" Probably one never feels completely Italian or American. I accepted both of my identities, but what does it mean? Do two identities with time carry the same weight and embody the same values? In the first few years here, home was not the Bronx but Benevento where I grew up with my family. My ethnic roots had not descended yet into American soil; they were still green-white-red. One did not come from two equal halves. As I approach old age, is my being composed of two parts that are inversely proportionate? The two parts of my being one on each side of the hyphen dwell in me like siblings, still occasionally sparring, one outshining the other depending on the day and the occasion. But as siblings they are intimately familiar with one another, intertwined. Nevertheless, to Italians I am clearly the *Americano*.

The immigrant's journey, no matter how ultimately rewarding, is founded on departure and arrival, on losses and gains. Having a dual identity has been an asset, allowing me to interact with and learn from a broad spectrum of fellow human beings. I also realize that having a dual identity can also be somewhat problematic, a liability.

Walking on the *Corso*, we had approached the area that had been in a state of rubble for many years from the bombings of World War II. They had finally rebuilt the Duomo that had been destroyed during the war. My father had always told stories about the beauty of that church and the huge bronze doors that the Nazis took to Germany. There it was now, rebuilt in all its majesty. I entered with my wife and girls, and we were in awe of its size. But it did not touch me; there were no personal memories: no baptisms, no first communion, no confirmations, no weddings, no big feasts, not even funerals that would say that there was something of me that remained there. I found the environment very cold, something very unusual for me, having always been a devout Catholic.

I felt the need for some spiritual reflection, but *that* was not the place. So I took my family to Madonna delle Grazie, the church that had the biggest feast of the year where my family had participated in so many celebrations. A flood of memories returned to me. I always remember that church packed with people. Most of the time we had to stand for the high Masses. It was in that church that I had my first moment of glory, the only moment of great pleasure of my childhood and youth. I received on the altar, during the high Mass in celebration of the feast of the Madonna, a meaningful recognition. One year in the early 1950s, the schools had a competition for the *Anno Mariano* on the meaning of the Madonna in our lives, for which the top three compositions submitted would be award a prize. I received the second prize, thanks to my mother.

Although my mother had only a third-grade education, she had an exceptional imagination and an extraordinary sensibility. I am sure that many other kids got help from their mothers, most of them with an education beyond that of my mother, but she received the second prize for the province of Benevento. She practically dictated the composition spontaneously to me. Her profound faith was always inspirational, but she had a great ability to converse informally, too; she was a raconteur who could persuasively tell a story. I felt embarrassed to receive the second prize for something that I did not write, but I felt proud that my mother with a third-grade education enabled me to win a prize when I was in eighth grade! There I was on the altar, on the occasion of the biggest feast around, with standing room only, receiving an award from the bishop. At the end of the Mass acquaintances of the family, so many people, came over to say *congratulazioni* and *bravo*. And many ladies kissed me for having used such wonderful words for Our Lady. In presenting the prize, they read a few lines from the composition, and I too felt that those were very touching words.

It was the beginning of July and I was wearing a new pair of shorts that my Uncle Egidio had his tailor make for me from the remnant material of his suit. My mother had bought me a new pair of shoes and I was ready for my public appearance. If the ceremony had taken place at a different time of the year, a suit would have been appropriate for the occasion, but it would have been unlikely that I would have had one. I got my first suit when I was eighteen; I wore it for special occasions and I took good care of it as one of the most precious things I owned.

Before going back home, I passed by the railroad station to show my girls the Strega factory, were the liquor that brought some commercial recognition to my city was produced. It could be found also in New York. Passing the station I remembered the two times I had taken the train before leaving for the United States. When I was about ten or eleven, I went with my mother on a pilgrimage to the Madonna of Montevergine. It was an incredible trip for the novelty of traveling. I did not sit for a second during the almost ninety minutes of travel. I stood with my face glued to the window and looked out onto the landscape, the people working in the fields, the villages on hilltops. There I was, in the very train that so many times I had seen in the distance from my house and had made me wonder where it was going and where it was taking people. Now on the train, I was still wondering how each trip could be different; always revealing something new.

The only other time I had taken the train before leaving for the United States was when I was sixteen and had to go to Caserta for the Air Force Academy physical. One day, going home from school I saw an announcement posted on one of the city billboards about enlisting in the Air Force Academy, and the picture of flying planes attracted my attention. I read the announcement and saw that I met the requirements to apply. I did not take down the information on how to apply or where to send the papers. Going home, I started to fantasize about finding a way out of the crowded conditions at home and how to obtain a free education for myself. I knew that it would be impossible for me to pursue studies at a university because of our financial condition. It is for this reason that I had just enrolled in a technical high school. Once I graduated, I had the skills to enter the work force. My brother Enrico had enrolled in the *liceo* and then had to go to a university to enter a profession. He too, had tried to find an escape from home by applying for the school for *sotto-ufficiale* of the *carabinieri*, the state police. But not having any political pull, he was not accepted.

His experience did not dampen my enthusiasm to seek future opportunities. The next day I went back to the billboard and copied down the information about the papers that were needed and addresses where they were to be mailed. I put the papers together, I asked my father to sign the application, and mailed them. For a couple of months I dreamed of being a pilot. For someone who didn't even have a bicycle and whose family had neither a motorcycle nor a car, it was very exciting to think of being in the cockpit of a plane and flying at will. I also liked to imagine myself in a nice uniform, a striking hat, and receiving attention from an attractive girl. Strangely enough, I never thought that I was going to be trained to fight in an airplane. After all, I was going to be an officer of the Italian Air Force. We had been waiting in vain for our visas to the United States for two years and the youngest in the family, Agnese, had just been born. I didn't feel that I should continue to take food from the table of my family, even though it was never scarce. The Air Force offered a good opportunity to test my future and, at the same time, make room at home.

When I received the letter in which they called me for a physical, I was in ecstasy. My dreams became incessant; I even took the liberty of telling my plans to a couple of close friends. No one was shocked or even surprised. In those days, there was a silent revolution on the part of the children of farmers and the working class to try to find a new path for our lives. Many children at school were similarly dreaming of ways to achieve a better social status.

The day I had to leave for the exam, I got up early and prepared for my first trip away from home on my own. I didn't take much for a three-day stay; on the other hand, I did not have much. My parents came out to see me leave, and both exhorted me to be careful, above all, not to be trapped by anyone ill-intentioned. My mother kissed me on my head and gave me the usual *Dio ti benedica*. It was not an emotional departure; I was going to be back in three days, hopefully with good news. But deep down I was nervous mainly because I had never taken a train by myself. Going to the station, about a five-mile walk, I was concerned about purchasing the ticket, figuring out the right track, the train to take, where to get off. It was all unknown to me.

But at the station everything was much easier than I expected. I asked where to wait for the train to Caserta and stood there impatiently. Once aboard, probably by a miracle, I found myself with a group of young men from the Apulia region—Barletta, Foggia, Bari, Brindisi—who, were going to Caserta for the same physical test. It was a great relief—I had company. It was the first time we were meeting, but bonds developed quickly. We had the same plan, the same hopes, the same dreams, and were feeling the same trepidation. Talking, we discovered that we had the same background and that there was something wrong in our society. Suddenly one of them, the most talkative, jumped on a seat and started to give voice to our reflections more or less with these words: "*Compagni*, here is the new Italy, the democratic *Italia* of the republic. No work and no prospects for a decent future for the children of the working class. Our best opportunity is to join in the army. Five thousand applicants for four hundred positions. And they tell us that we must be happy because Italy is changing profoundly."

Addressing us as "*Compagni*" left me a bit perplexed because in political jargon it meant comrades, and was the greeting used by Socialists and Communists when they met. But *compagni* meant also "friends" and "classmates," and I did not know how to interpret him. As we proceeded on our trip and continued chatting, it became clear that the fellow had a mature political awareness, and so did the other boys, especially those from the cities. I was absorbing all this with great interest. It was clear that our different circumstances were making us learn fast creating a great sense of social awareness and common sense.

When the train arrived at Caserta, we discovered that there were many more boys on the other cars headed to the same destination. We arrived at the Royal Palace and checked in. We were given a sack with our bed sheets, bed cover, and pillow with a warning that we were responsible for it and at the end of our stay we had to hand it in at checkout. I took the warning lightly because no one would have imagined stealing a sheet to take home. In groups we went to different rooms where there were about twenty beds in each. As instructed, we made our beds and then we proceeded to the dining hall for lunch.

The meal was nothing great but probably more balanced than what I normally had home: first serving with second dish, vegetables, and fruit. Some of the guys made negative comments about the overcooked pasta, the taste of the meat, the tasteless vegetables, and everything else. I had the impression that some of those who were complaining were those that had less at home but were complaining to create the impression that they weren't poor and that their mothers were excellent cooks. I was finding myself in a new landscape. I was a farm kid from a family of eight children who was used to eating whatever was on the table. We never criticized the meals and if we did not like a dish, my mother was not going to provide an alternate. I guess you develop the ability to criticize when you know that there are alternatives. Farm kids, used to fewer alternatives or no alternatives at all, customarily complain and whine less than others.

We spent the evening being briefed about the academy, the course of studies, the expectations of the school, the thrill of being a cadet, but also the high demands of the program. We listened with great interest and were anxious to go through the physical. We knew that many of us had to be eliminated. The first selection came with the physical. Those who were declared fit were going to be called for the academic test; the best were going to be accepted to the academy. We had developed a degree of friendship and were enjoying the newly formed relationships. However, we also saw each other with a certain suspicion because we were competing for a very limited number of places and many of us were not going to be accepted.

The next morning we had breakfast and then we were led into different rooms and were briefed on how to prepare for the physical. The officer who lined up our group was very emphatic about the cleanliness of our bodies. "You need to take a shower before the physical. You must make sure that you are very clean when you present yourselves before the Medical Captain. Remember, you have two heads, the top and the bottom. Make sure that the bottom head is very clean. If you show a dirty head, you will be automatically sent home." There was certainly need to have a shower. Most people in 1956 did not have a shower in their homes. I, and I assume most of the boys, had taken a sponge bath before leaving and were relatively clean. The problem was the lower head. The great majority of boys had not been circumcised and the potential to have the "lower head" dirty was high.

As any man can imagine, it was an unreal scene to see those boys under the shower taking care of the lower head. Such a precious part of the body suddenly had become a worry; it could take on the aspect of life or death. There they were shining it to make it presentable to the Captain. Is it possible that it was the part of the body that was going to receive the most scrutiny?

We were lined up, as we were, naked and one by one passed in front the Captain for a preliminary checkup. When my turn came, I proceeded with the routine physical. "Are you related to Major Mignone, originally from Beltiglio?" the Captain asked. Beltiglio was a neighborhood close to the village of my birth. "I don't think so," I responded. "My family has never talked about or mentioned a family member being a Major in the Air Force."

After we dressed, we went to lunch with the same food and the same complaints from the same kids who had complained the day before. We were going through the various phases of our physical tests but I noticed that the comradeship weakening. The tension of competition, over which we did not have control, and the anxiety of pending eliminations dampened our spirits.

When I went to the room where my bed was, I noticed that a sheet was missing from my bed. I was shocked. Was someone playing a trick? Did someone want to make fun of me? The next day we were leaving and I had to hand in the *biancheria* received at the checkout. Without thinking twice, almost instinctively, I made sure that no one would see me and grabbed a sheet from another bed and put it on mine.

Next day the verdict came. I had been eliminated with hundreds of other kids. It was not pleasant news. There went my dreams of being an officer in the Air Force. On the train, some boys cursed the bureaucratic system, others complained about the lack of jobs, the social injustice, the corruption—many kids felt that only those who had the right political pull made it. I was cursing myself for the way I responded to the Captain about the possible existence of a family relative Major in the Air Force. That could have been my recommendation. I should have said, "Yes, Sir. That's my uncle." But it was too late. Having grown up on a farm my instinct for lying was not fast enough for living in a complex society where personal relations could create favoritism. I did not know those sets of rules that governed the social structures and culture of bureaucratic systems in a culture ruled by nepotism, strong political ties, and loyalty. Probably the complaints and curses of those boys were well founded.

At Benevento's station I bade farewell to my new friends and got off the train. While stepping off, one of them screamed, "We need a revolution!" Walking home I was very disappointed, and that scream about the revolution was ringing in my head. I was wondering if I would ever make it. I just did not want to be stuck on the farm. My brother Enrico had tried to take off and had failed too. I became anxious to know who were going to be the 400 chosen, how many of them would be the children of farmers, shoemakers, barbers, carpenters, and day laborers? That would have told me if my hopes were in vain.

When I arrived home, my mother was certainly delighted to see me and anxious to know how it went. "Mom, hundreds of other boys and I were rejected," I said in an annoyed tone so that she would not ask the various "whys." She fried a couple of eggs and we had lunch. In the evening at dinner, my father wanted to know about the entire experience. To cut it short, I asked him about the Mignone Major in the Air Force. When he heard the story, he exploded with a series of expletives: *Cretino! Idiota! Stupido!* and everything else. "Couldn't you have said, 'He is my uncle or my father's cousin!' You are not quick thinking!" he said, very upset.

There was no question that I had made a mistake, but I had learned a lot. I had learned so much being in contact with those boys, and I pledged to myself to always use my experiences as lessons. Having to do things by myself created situations for mistakes, but I was able to learn from mistakes at an early age, and I was spared from making big mistakes in my later life. I learned quickly that lessons are not given, but taken.

Walking in the city, I did not reveal to my wife and daughters this story that had come to mind. I continued at school but the scream for a revolution from that boy on the train kept ringing in my mind. Now, walking with my family as a university professor in the footsteps of my youth, I thought that I had participated in a revolution, a different revolution than the one that boy had in mind. My future had been shaped by the "silent revolution" of emigration which had been undertaken by millions of other people. There was a sense of satisfaction in that walk, but I couldn't find happiness in what I was experiencing. Benevento had changed, my relatives had changed, people in general had changed, every thing had changed. Very often I would hear from people, "America is here." The country in a matter of a few years had changed profoundly. Mass urbanization, geographical mobility, schooling, conscription, and the diffusion of radio and television had broken many social and cultural barriers. Talking with young people I noticed that even the language had changed. Dialects were fading away. The development of industries engaged in production, re-production, and distribution of cultural products had brought in their wake an anthropological revolution, a break-up of old ideo-logies and class identities, and a new cultural homogenization. Probably the revolution of my newly found friend on the train had taken place without spilling blood.

But I was perplexed to find a different Italy. Did modernization "denature" Italian culture by breaking up its traditions of regional differentiation? Was Italy going through a beneficial transfor-mation on every level? I could not figure out if modernization had standardized and leveled cultural consumption or brought with it new forms of cultural distinction. American soap operas present-ed on the Italian state television had been creeping into the priva-cy of Italian homes and at the same time brought Italians into the private homes of Americans. The effect had been strong, especial-ly on the younger generation. The children of my relatives and friends were revealing the same elastic behavior and attitudes of our American youth: gathering in gangs, wearing jeans and tennis shoes, riding motorbikes, wearing basketball jackets with large superscriptions on their backs.

It was certainly gratifying to see how fast Italians had radically improved their ways of life. The American way of living had pen-etrated especially working-class homes. Italy had turned into a consumer society along American lines. Moreover, America had become a model of behavior especially for the young generation. Old moral values and traditional behavior had been replaced by a relaxed, looser way of life. I did not know if Italy was living in a golden age or a time of moral disintegration and cultural turmoil.

It was clear that when we emigrate we must leave permanent-ly and pursue our own destiny wholeheartedly. It is impossible to expect that things will remain the same. What was mine was gone. The threads were broken. We can never return; even when we vis-it places that have been part of our lives, we must never give in to nostalgia.

SIXTEEN

As I have aged I have become kinder and less critical of myself. I have become my own friend. I have seen members of the family and too many dear friends leave this world too soon, before they understood the great freedom that comes with aging. I know sometimes I am forgetful, but there again, there are parts of life that are better forgotten and I eventually remember the important things. Surely, over the years, my heart has been broken. How can your heart not break when you lose loved ones, or a child suffers? But, broken hearts are what give us strength, understanding, and compassion. A heart never broken is pristine and sterile and will never know the joy of being imperfect or fully appreciate the joy of achievements. How can we fully appreciate the day without knowing the night, the sunset without the sunrise, the meaning of a full stomach without having suffered hunger; how can we understand the joy of Paradise without knowing the presence of Hell?

I am so blessed to have lived long enough to have my hair, whatever is left on my head, turn gray. As you get older, it is easier to be positive. You care less about what other people think and say. I don't question myself so much anymore. I like being old. It has set me free. I like being the person I have become. I am not going to live forever. But while I am still living, I will not waste time lamenting what could have been, or worrying about what will be.

Basically my siblings and I feel very satisfied with our emigrant experience and our modest accomplishments. We integrated well into American society. We became part of America's remarkable history of welcoming and assimilating immigrants. In a way we represented, as millions of other immigrants, the positive result of American human-capital development. As did millions of other immigrants we enriched the human capital of the American workplace. In our case also, the education system was the place where most of the human capital was actually generated and transformed. Education was a very productive investment that America made in us, and it will yield high returns for all immigrants to follow. Our experience reaffirmed American social egalitarianism; despite the existence at all times of great disparities of income and wealth in our society, Americans really do believe that "all men are created equal," that no one is intrinsically any better than anyone else, and that every newborn American child should have the same shot at opportunity and success. The inspired civic model and individualistic and egalitarian values of the United States helped us reach "the promised land." Paradoxically we had to become poorer in order to become richer.

My family, like millions of others, like the Chinese, Indian, and Korean immigrant families today continue to be imported human capital that has always been one of the strongest assets of American society. Every one of America's most successful groups has a superiority complex, a deep-seated belief in its own exceptional capabilities. Jews, Mormons, American Iranians, Asians, Nigerians, all believe themselves to be unique in their ability to achieve. When they are young their parents express less satisfaction with their academic achievements than average American parents. There are inner dynamics, sets of values and beliefs, habits and practices, that individuals from any background can make a part of their lives and their children's lives that will enable them to pursue success as they themselves define it. Probably fear of being looked down on, a perception of peril, feelings of inadequacy, and the fear, conscious or unconscious of losing the road to success pushes immigrants to work harder. To be an immigrant is almost, by definition, to be insecure — an experience of deep economic and social anxiety, of not knowing whether you can earn a living or give your children a decent life. Being simultaneously insecure and desiring to make it creates a potent tension.

Immigrants usually have a predisposition to fight obstacles and endure hardships. My family, as all other immigrants, had an innate ability to resist temptation, especially the temptation to give up in the face of hardship or quit instead of persevering at difficult tasks. We, as immigrants, constantly demonstrate that upward mobility is not dead and the American dream is alive and well.

We did not have money and we did not have work when we arrived here. We all went to college, undergraduate and graduate studies, and no one graduated with a penny of debt. It seems unreal in the world of today where 66 percent (in 2008) of undergraduate students have school loans that average $27,803 by the time they graduate. Students are drowning in debt. One problem is that often parents don't have the same feelings, the same disposition to sacrifice for their children. Most of them are not able or willing to prioritize their options in favor of helping to pay for the education of their children and make an investment in their future. They don't like the idea of forgoing a vacation or dinner out several times a week or not replacing a car that still runs well. My siblings and I, following the traditional ideas and ideals of our parents, did not compromise when it came to the education of our children. We paid every penny of their education costs for them and permitted them to go to the best universities that accepted them. We were able to accomplish it through the cooperation, sacrifices, and guidance that our spouses provided. The results were best where that chemistry worked to perfection.

When our children reached their teenage years, my wife brought up the issue of "allowance" for the children. I responded, curious, "What's that?" She understood and never brought up the issue again. I made my children understand that our financial resources were limited, and that if I spent money for nonessential things, there was going to be less money for their education and for their weddings. My wife set the lead by her example, and the children followed. All three of our daughters worked to earn their spending money.

I like to say that my children were like gold, and I mean it in every sense of the word. We were always open and spoke to them candidly and made them part of all our family affairs. Sometimes they grumbled, but they always obeyed. A couple of times I reminded them that I was born during a devastating war, that I was the second of eight children and that I was an immigrant. Even if they sometimes felt that I was too demanding, they tolerated me. While they were growing up, I always spent part of the summer away teaching and never worried about them. In fact, I never lost any sleep worrying about my children. Pamela took care of our lawn from the time she was thirteen years old. When she went to college, Cristina took over, and after her it was Elizabeth's turn.

My siblings, for the most part, used the same approach with their children. They always had a candid dialogue with them while teaching them responsibility, discipline, self-control, strictness, and perseverance. The older siblings were probably stricter and more demanding; the immigrant experiences of the younger ones may have been fading. Nevertheless, all our children were brought up respecting and using the old values. They were not pampered, doted upon, helmeted, bubble-wrapped, or otherwise protected from the cold, cruel world for long. They were never made to believe that the world revolved around them. We never worried that their self-esteem would suffer if teachers graded their papers with a red marker. And as athletes, we never believed that they should have received a trophy just for showing up.

In 1996 our children started to branch out. Of my parents' twenty-eight grandchildren my daughter Pamela was the first to marry. It became immediately clear that we were not going to remain attached to our ethnic purity or insularity. Pamela married Daniel, a Jew. When they were getting serious our major concern was how the Hollywood culture of Daniel's family had affected their family values. But Daniel's grandparents had been married for practically the same number of years as Pamela's grandparents and most importantly, their family relationships were strong.

Whenever the prospect of marriage was shaping up for the grandchildren, family background and family values were checked. In fact, for the other twenty-seven children, who are well established in our society as lawyers, doctors, university professors, teachers, prosecutors, a CEO, etc., family considerations have been central in their choices. In the numerous intermarriages — Jewish, Portuguese, Indian, Irish, German, Croatian — the unions have always been made focusing on family stability. And most have stayed near home. Except for three of them, all the grandchildren established their families within a radius of thirty miles.

The family can be a powerful unit if it is united behind a shared set of goals and family values. We did it without adopting a family mission statement or a family constitution or strategic plan or code of conduct, as a valuable first step toward uniting everyone in a family around goals and the actions needed to make them a reality. In our family we didn't have to look for ways to ensure that future generations would inherit values along with money, or seek to build a philanthropic legacy. Our family didn't have to worry about all that. Our unifying cement was getting behind a shared purpose that strengthened the bonds within the family and also guided the family and individual members through daily and major life decisions to help realize its goals. We were all part of the same goal.

That way of working was an ideal way that taught us financial and socially responsible decision-making at a young age We all knew what our family aspirations as a whole were. Our family values ranged from overarching characteristics — integrity, strong work ethic, giving back — to more personal, experience-based considerations. We all knew that there are plenty of ways that money can get in the way of growth and development. Being clear on the purpose of money in our family helped ensure that didn't happen.

We learned how to work for the common good and that the common good is to be found not in the discovery of new principles for living, but in the *rediscovery* of well-tested truths about the importance of faith, life, and family. Values are "caught rather than taught." Fortunately many families in America are not what we watch coming from Hollywood lately; in millions of families, including our children's young families, parents do teach their children traditional family values just as our parents taught us. Unfortunately though, too many of those who get married quickly get divorced, and too many American children are born into broken homes.

In my family we all thank God for having given us a strong family, a family in which my father and mother were totally committed to each other in a lifelong, loving relationship. There was never any question about this in my mind, never any thought that my parents would separate, never any talk of divorce. It was, and is, a "till death do us part" kind of relationship. So I was born into what has been called a "natural family" with a father and a mother and their children. Traditional family values require respect for others, especially for one's elders who are the living repositories of such values. I was taught to respect not just my parents and grandparents but all of my elders.

And everything starts at a young age. In our early years my sibling and I were home-schooled. Every traditional family is a school of love and life and virtue. Growing up, my parents insisted that we keep a regular daily schedule: Wake up and go to school, try your best at school, come home and do chores on the farm, complete our homework, and join the family at dinner, and only then, if there was time left, relax and enjoy free time. It is from such good practices that good habits are formed and from such good habits that good character is molded.

Take our work ethic. Growing up there was always work to be done — grass to be cut for the animals, cows to be fed, tobacco to be taken care of, and so on. I may have complained about these chores when I was younger — in fact, I am sure that I did — but I have come to be grateful. From them I have learned a work ethic that helped me to be successful in whatever I attempted in life.

My mother seemed to have endless amounts of patience. My father instead reacted with punishments. The two different approaches were never in conflict or seen as contradicting each other. We had much less trouble with other traditional values, such as the need to always tell the truth and to respect the property of others. I was told never to lie and never to steal. I rarely did, since the truth of these values seemed to me to be self-evident. It seems as clear to me today as it did when I was younger that stealing and lying are simply wrong. I believe that these and other traditional values are written on the human heart. They were certainly inscribed in my family code. From my mother we learned love, empathy, and kindness towards others. From my father we have learned humility, selflessness, self-control, and a strong work ethic.

Learning those values at a young age allows you to understand that such values are fundamental to the good life and must be integral parts of our character. I believe that this is so because there are some values, chiefly those that are laid down in the Ten Commandments, which are also written on the human heart and help us in shaping our civil and civic living. It's important to remember this: Every person has multiple opportunities to be part of a traditional family. There is the family you were born into, the family that you form upon marriage, and the families that your children form when they marry. My siblings and I have been lucky that for the most part we were able to pass along these traditional values and feel more secure to build a better future

I sometimes worry how the family grandchildren are bringing up their children because of the way they pamper them and mollify their desires so easily, even before they are born. In a few years, some of them, in pursuit of the fame they crave more than anything else, will be auditioning for musical talent shows. I am afraid that, if the judges reject them, they will defiantly respond: "That's your opinion!" Others are going to apply for jobs and may brazenly ask the interviewer if there is a shortcut to the executive suite. I still believe that the strongest steel comes from the hottest fire.

I am afraid that our younger generation will not care if the world does not see them as special. What will matter is that they see themselves that way. I hope that I am wrong. I pray that I am wrong. But I already see this with the younger hires today in academia; they arrive asking for entitlements and don't want to spend a penny of their own for their professional advancement. As they go through life, our grandchildren will find obstacles and may fail. And some may fail because they don't have the resilience to fight. For generations, accomplishments were attained if one could but persevere and press on—that force of will shaped our character and determined our destiny. My grandchildren and the children of their generation don't need the excessive coddling. What they need is straight talk and a reality check.

We did not become a powerful nation through hope and soft backs rather than self-reliance. We cherish freedom and the absence of restrictions on our ability to think and to act; but the corollary of freedom is individual responsibility. A great Italian humanist, Pico della Mirandola, said that man has been endowed with a greater sense of dignity than the angels: Angels can only be angels, but man can be a brute or a semi-god. Freedom is great if it translates our desires in the capacity for self-determination that is not a given entity but a condition, and conditions change. We hope that our grandchildren and their generation will have the resilience, the fortitude, the skills and the knowledge, the creativity, and the character to aim to be semi-gods.

ABOUT THE AUTHOR

Mario B. Mignone emigrated to the US in 1960. He received his BA from City College (CUNY), MA and PhD from Rutgers University and began his teaching career at Stony Brook in 1970, where he is now SUNY Distinguished Service Professor and Director of the Center for Italian Studies.

As Director of the Center, he created the Alfonse M. D'Amato Chair in Italian and Italian American Studies, the first endowed chair in the Stony Brook College of Arts and Sciences, and endowments for a full fellowship and two lecture series. For over twenty-five years Professor Mignone has been editor of *Forum Italicum*, one of the most prestigious journals of Italian Studies, and editor of Filibrary, a book series. As an accomplished author, he has written numerous books and more than fifty scholarly articles on modern Italian literature and culture.

His books cover a wide range topics of Italian literature and culture: *Pirandello in America; Columbus Meeting of Cultures; Homage to Moravia; Il teatro di Eduardo De Filippo; Anormalità e angoscia nella narrativa di Dino Buzzati; Eduardo De Filippo; Italy Today: At the Crossroads of the New Millennium* and *Italy Today: Facing the Challenges of the New Millennium*. In 2013, Professor Mignone was invited by Library of Congress to write the essays for an important book on the Italian American Experience: *Explorers, Emigrants, Citizens: A Visual History of the Italian American Experience from the Collections of the Library of Congress*. Passionate about immersing students in the full Italian experience, he started several exchange programs with the University of Rome "La Sapienza," University of Messina, LUMSA, and Florence University of the Arts.

In recognition of his extraordinary professional service and scholarly work, he was appointed member of the SUNY Distinguished Academy; he has received many honors, including *Cavaliere Ufficiale al merito della Repubblica*, bestowed by the president of the Italian Republic; he was appointed by the Governor of New York to the SUNY College Council at Old Westbury, and serves on the Advisory Board of Florence University of the Arts.

VIA FOLIOS

A refereed book series dedicated to the culture of Italians and Italian Americans.

Bordighera Press is an imprint of Bordighera, Incorporated, an independently owned not-for-profit scholarly organization that has no legal affiliation with the University of Central Florida or with The John D. Calandra Italian American Institute, Queens College/CUNY.

History, $12

PAOLO RUFFILLI, *Dark Room/Camera oscura*, Vol. 66, Poetry, $11

HELEN BAROLINI, *Crossing the Alps*, Vol. 65, Fiction, $14

COSMO FERRARA, *Profiles of Italian Americans*, Vol. 64, Italian Americana, $16

GIL FAGIANI, *Chianti in Connecticut*, Vol. 63, Poetry, $10

BASSETTI & D'ACQUINO, *Italic Lessons*, Vol. 62, Italian/American Studies, $10

CAVALIERI & PASCARELLI, Eds., *The Poet's Cookbook*, Vol. 61, Poetry/Recipes, $12

EMANUEL DI PASQUALE, *Siciliana*, Vol. 60, Poetry, $8

NATALIA COSTA, Ed., *Bufalini*, Vol. 59, Poetry. $18.

RICHARD VETERE, *Baroque*, Vol. 58, Fiction. $18.

LEWIS TURCO, *La Famiglia/The Family*, Vol. 57, Memoir, $15

NICK JAMES MILETI, *The Unscrupulous*, Vol. 56, Humanities, $20

BASSETTI, ACCOLLA, D'AQUINO, *Italici: An Encounter with Piero Bassetti*, Vol. 55, Italian Studies, $8

GIOSE RIMANELLI, *The Three-legged One*, Vol. 54, Fiction, $15

CHARLES KLOPP, *Bele Antiche Stòrie*, Vol. 53, Criticism, $25

JOSEPH RICAPITO, *Second Wave*, Vol. 52, Poetry, $12

GARY MORMINO, *Italians in Florida*, Vol. 51, History, $15

GIANFRANCO ANGELUCCI, *Federico F.*, Vol. 50, Fiction, $15

ANTHONY VALERIO, *The Little Sailor*, Vol. 49, Memoir, $9

ROSS TALARICO, *The Reptilian Interludes*, Vol. 48, Poetry, $15

RACHEL GUIDO DE VRIES, *Teeny Tiny Tino's Fishing Story*, Vol. 47, Children's Literature, $6

EMANUEL DI PASQUALE, *Writing Anew*, Vol. 46, Poetry, $15

MARIA FAMÀ, *Looking For Cover*, Vol. 45, Poetry, $12

ANTHONY VALERIO, *Toni Cade Bambara's One Sicilian Night*, Vol. 44, Poetry, $10

EMANUEL CARNEVALI, Dennis Barone, Ed., *Furnished Rooms*, Vol. 43, Poetry, $14

BRENT ADKINS, et al., Ed., *Shifting Borders, Negotiating Places*, Vol. 42, Proceedings, $18

GEORGE GUIDA, *Low Italian*, Vol. 41, Poetry, $11

GARDAPHÈ, GIORDANO, TAMBURRI, *Introducing Italian Americana*, Vol. 40, Italian/American Studies, $10

DANIELA GIOSEFFI, *Blood Autumn/Autunno di sangue*, Vol. 39, Poetry, $15/$25

FRED MISURELLA, *Lies to Live by*, Vol. 38, Stories, $15

STEVEN BELLUSCIO, *Constructing a Bibliography*, Vol. 37, Italian Americana, $15

ANTHONY JULIAN TAMBURRI, Ed., *Italian Cultural Studies 2002*, Vol. 36, Essays, $18

BEA TUSIANI, *con amore*, Vol. 35, Memoir, $19

FLAVIA BRIZIO-SKOV, Ed., *Reconstructing Societies in the Aftermath of War*, Vol. 34, History, $30

TAMBURRI, et al., Eds., *Italian Cultural Studies 2001*, Vol. 33, Essays, $18

ELIZABETH G. MESSINA, Ed., *In Our Own Voices*, Vol. 32, Italian/American Studies, $25

STANISLAO G. PUGLIESE, *Desperate Inscriptions*, Vol. 31, History, $12

HOSTERT & TAMBURRI, Eds., *Screening Ethnicity*, Vol. 30, Italian/American Culture, $25

G. PARATI & B. LAWTON, Eds., *Italian Cultural Studies*, Vol. 29, Essays, $18

HELEN BAROLINI, *More Italian Hours*, Vol. 28, Fiction, $16

FRANCO NASI, Ed., *Intorno alla Via Emilia*, Vol. 27, Culture, $16

ARTHUR L. CLEMENTS, *The Book of Madness & Love*, Vol. 26, Poetry, $10

JOHN CASEY, et al., *Imagining Humanity*, Vol. 25, Interdisciplinary Studies, $18

ROBERT LIMA, *Sardinia/Sardegna*, Vol. 24, Poetry, $10

DANIELA GIOSEFFI, *Going On*, Vol. 23, Poetry, $10

ROSS TALARICO, *The Journey Home*, Vol. 22, Poetry, $12

EMANUEL DI PASQUALE, *The Silver Lake Love Poems*, Vol. 21, Poetry, $7

JOSEPH TUSIANI, *Ethnicity*, Vol. 20, Poetry, $12

CPSIA information can be obtained
at www.ICGtesting.com
Printed in the USA
FSOW02n0642100915
10770FS